Hope Finders

13 Fun Filled Bible Lessons About Hope

Susan L. Lingo

Standard Publishing
Cincinnati, Ohio

DEDICATION

**Then you will know that I am the Lord;
those who hope in me will not be disappointed.
Isaiah 49:23**

Hope Finders
© 2001 Susan L. Lingo

Published by Standard Publishing, Cincinnati, Ohio
A division of Standex International Corporation

All rights reserved. No part of this book may be reproduced in any manner whatsoever without written permission from the publisher, except where noted in the text and in the case of brief quotations embodied in critical articles and reviews.

Credits
   Produced by Susan L. Lingo, Bright Ideas Books™
   Cover design by Diana Walters
   Illustrated by Marilynn G. Barr and Megan E. Jeffery

All Scripture quotations, unless otherwise indicated, are taken from the HOLY BIBLE, NEW INTERNATIONAL VERSION®. NIV®. Copyright © 1973, 1978, 1984 by International Bible Society. Used by permission of Zondervan Publishing House. All rights reserved.

08 07 06 05 04   5 4 3 2
ISBN 0-7847-1235-2
Printed in the United States of America

CONTENTS

Introduction 4
Teacher Feature: Choosing Great Kids' Resources 7

SECTION 1: GOD'S GIFT OF HOPE

A Perfect Foundation (Isaiah 40:31; 49:23; Jeremiah 14:22; Romans 15:4, 13) **12**
A Heavenly Hope (Isaiah 42:1-4; Luke 2:4-14; Titus 1:2; 1 Peter 1:3) **20**
A Spirit of Hope (Romans 8:9, 14, 16; 1 Corinthians 2:12; Galatians 5:5) **28**

SECTION 2: HOPE FOR TOMORROW

Faith in the Future (Psalms 33:11; 131:3; Jeremiah 29:11; Ephesians 2:10) **38**
Saving Grace (Romans 5:6, 8; 8:2; 2 Thessalonians 2:16; 17; Titus 3:3-7) **46**
Home of Hope (John 14:1-3; 1 Peter 1:3, 4; 2 Peter 3:13; Revelation 21:11-21) **54**

SECTION 3: HOPE FOR TODAY

The Hope Rope (Psalms 18:6; 33:20; Lamentations 3:21-23; Hebrews 6:19) **64**
Hearts of Hope (Psalms 25:5; 33:20, 21; Romans 12:10-13; 2 Thessalonians 2:16, 17) .. **72**
A Helping of Hope (Romans 12:13; 2 Corinthians 9:8; 1 Timothy 3:13) **80**

SECTION 4: THE ASSURANCE OF HOPE

It's a Sure Thing! (Psalm 71:14; Jeremiah 31:17; Micah 7:7; Hebrews 11:1) **90**
A Light in Darkness (Romans 4:18-24; 2 Corinthians 4:4, 6-9; 2 Timothy 3:12) **98**
Target: Hope! (Psalms 27:14; 33:20, 21; 130:5; Romans 5:3-5; Jude 21) **106**

HOPE FINDERS REVIEW LESSON (Isaiah 40:31; Lamentations 3:21-23) **116**

Introduction

INTRODUCTION

POWERING UP YOUR KIDS' FAITH!

Congratulations! You are about to embark on a wonderful and powerful mission to strengthen, energize, and stabilize your kids' faith and fundamental knowledge of God—faith and fundamentals that will launch your kids powerfully into the twenty-first century!

Hope Finders is part of the Power Builders Series, an exciting and powerfully effective curriculum that includes *Faith Finders, Servant Leaders, Disciple Makers, Value Seekers, Peace Makers, Joy Builders, Power Boosters,* and the book you're now holding. *Hope Finders* is dedicated to exploring where hope comes from in an oftentimes hopeless world and how God promises us the assurance of hope today and for all our tomorrows. Thirteen theme-oriented lessons help your kids explore, assess, and apply God's truths about discovering hope and sharing hope with others. And woven throughout each lesson is Scripture, Scripture, and more Scripture!

Each lesson in *Hope Finders* has the following features:

POWER FOCUS (Approximate time: 10 minutes)—You'll begin with a mighty motivator to get kids thinking about the focus of the lesson. This may include an eye-popping devotion, a simple game, or another lively attention-getting tool. Also included are interactive discussion and a brief overview of what kids will be learning during the lesson. *Purpose: To focus attention and cue kids in to what they'll be learning during the lesson.*

MIGHTY MESSAGE (Approximate time: 15 minutes)—This is the body of the lesson and includes engaging Bible passages that actively teach about the lesson's theme. The Mighty Message is not just "another Bible story," so your kids will discover God's truths through powerful passages and important portions of Scripture that are supported by additional verses and made relevant to kids' lives. Processing questions help kids explore each side of the passages and their relation to the theme, beginning with easier questions for young children and ending with

Introduction

more challenging think-about-it questions for older kids. Meaty and memorable, this
lesson section will help kids learn tremendous truths! *Purpose: To teach powerful biblical truths and offer thought-provoking discussion in age-appropriate ways.*

MESSAGE IN MOTION (Approximate time: 10-15 minutes)—This section contains engaging activities that enrich and reinforce the lesson theme. It may include creative crafts, lively games and relays, action songs and rhythmic raps, mini service projects, and much more. *Purpose: To enrich learning in memorable and fun ways that build a sense of community.*

SUPER SCRIPTURE (Approximate time: 10-15 minutes)—This all-important section encourages and helps kids effectively learn, understand, and apply God's Word in their lives. The Mighty Memory Verse was chosen so every child can effectively learn it during the course of three weeks, but an extra-challenge verse is offered for older kids or children who can handle learning more verses. You are free to substitute your own choice of verses in this section, but please keep in mind that the activities, songs, crafts, and mnemonic devices are designed for the Mighty Memory Verse and the accompanying extra-challenge verse. And remember, when it comes to learning God's Word, effective learning takes place when kids work on only one or two verses over the course of several weeks! *Purpose: To memorize, learn, recall, and use God's Word.*

POWERFUL PROMISE (Approximate time: 5-10 minutes)—The lesson closes with a summary, a promise, and a prayer. You'll summarize the lesson, the Mighty Memory Verse, and the theme, then challenge kids to make a special commitment to God for the coming week. The commitments are theme-related and give kids a chance to put their faith into action. Finally, a brief prayer and responsive farewell blessing end the lesson. *Purpose: To make a commitment of faith to God and express thanks and praise to him.*

POWER PAGE! (Take-home paper)—Each lesson ends with a fun-to-do take-along page that encourages kids to keep the learning going at home. Scripture puzzles, crafts, recipes, games, Bible read-about-its, Mighty Memory Verse reinforcement, and more challenge kids through independent discovery and learning fun. *Purpose: To reinforce, review, and enrich the day's lesson and the Mighty Memory Verse.*

PLUS, in every Power Builder's book you'll discover these great features!
★ **WHIZ QUIZZES!** At the end of each section is a reproducible Whiz Quiz to

Introduction

gently, yet effectively, assess what has been learned. Completed by kids in about five minutes at the end of lessons 3, 6, 9, and 12, the Whiz Quiz is a nonthreatening and fun measuring tool to allow teachers, kids, and parents to actually see what has been learned in the prior weeks. When kids complete each Whiz Quiz, consider presenting them a collectible surprise such as a vase and silk flowers that represent how God's hope is growing and flowering in their lives. For example, after the first Whiz Quiz, present each child with a small bud vase. After the next Whiz Quiz, present a red silk flower. Then use blue and yellow flowers for lessons 9 and 12. When the book is complete, kids will have an entire bouquet to remind them of the way God's hope flowers in our lives even in the midst of seemingly hopeless situations. Kids will love the cool reminders of the lessons and their accomplishments! Be sure to keep children's completed Whiz Quiz pages in folders to present to kids at the end of the book or at the end of the year, in combination with other Whiz Quizzes from different books in the Power Builders Series.

★ **LESSON 13 REVIEW!** The last lesson in *Hope Finders* is an important review of all that's been learned, applied, accomplished, and achieved during the past twelve weeks. Kids will love the lively review games, action songs, unique review tools, and celebratory feel of this special lesson!

★ **SCRIPTURE STRIPS!** At the back of the book, you'll discover every Mighty Memory Verse and extra-challenge verse that appears in *Hope Finders*. These reproducible Scripture strips can be copied and cut apart to use over and over for crafts, games, cards, bookmarks, and other fun and fabulous "you-name-its"! Try gluing these strips to long Formica chips to make colorful, clattery key chains that double as super Scripture reviews!

★ **TEACHER FEATURE!** Discover timeless teaching tips and hints, hands-on help, and a whole lot more in this mini teacher workshop. Every book in the Power Builders series offers a unique Teacher Feature that helps leaders understand and teach through issues such as discipline, prayer, Scripture memory, and more. The Teacher Feature in *Hope Finders* is "Choosing Great Kids' Resources."

God bless you as you teach with patience, love, and this powerful resource to help launch kids into another century of love, learning, and serving God! More POWER to you!

Teacher Feature

CHOOSING GREAT KIDS' RESOURCES

Place three plants in front of you and look closely. Which plant seems strongest, healthiest, or most promising in bearing fruit or flowers? The differences may be difficult to discern, yet they are vital if your hope is to raise plants that produce beauty and bear the best fruit. A weekend naturalist may not know what to look for, but the accomplished agronomist knows the nuances that differentiate between beauty and blight, fruit and fruitless. All it takes is training and a careful eye. No, we're not about to embark on a planting course for petunias, but choosing the most effective children's programming materials and curriculum can be as confusing and certainly much more important! A solid curriculum or resource product can make the difference between blight and bounty in a child's spiritual life and day-to-day reactions and relationships. Let's examine the five crucial components to consider when choosing children's educational programming so the seeds of God's Word you plant in a child's heart and mind have the best chance of producing life-changing fruits!

GOALS. Personal and professional goal-setting is as common as the air we breathe. We want and need goals to aim for, dreams to yearn after, and a sense of purpose to add meaning to daily routines and work. If we never set goals, how would we know if anything was achieved? Goals are just as vital to learning as they are to our jobs. After all, kids' learning *is* their job! Yet educational goals and solid objectives tend to be the most overlooked area of children's programming. Solid, well-thought out lessons will always have a stated goal or goals to clue you in as to what kids will be learning. Educational objectives usually begin with verbs such as *explore, examine, discover, learn, discuss, understand,* and *express.* A good objective for a lesson about faith might be: *To explore how Jesus' resurrection helps us have faith in eternal life.* Unfortunately, lessons often have objectives that are little more than activity schedules and use words such as *make, play,* or *sing,* as in: *Kids will play a game about sharing.* Watch for carefully stated lesson objectives; they clue you into what kids will be learning and how "deep" the lesson will go.

Teacher Feature

Along with objectives go measurable tools to help identify what kids are truly learning. One way to measure learning is through behavior and choices, since kids who are truly hearing Christ's messages will model more positive behaviors and attitudes. Another way to measure if learning is truly taking place is through short, fun-to-complete quizzes, questionnaires, and review games. The Whiz Quiz pages included in the Power Builders Curriculum Series are fun tools that measure kids' learning, allow you to reteach areas that may need extra work, and communicate to parents how their kids are doing. And don't overlook the fact that kids enjoy seeing what they've learned!

BALANCE. Solid lessons and activities offer a great deal of balance between crucial areas of learning. Is a lesson or activity merely frenetic activity, or is there a time of more quiet discussion and contemplation? Do the lessons offer variety in learning styles, including visual, auditory, tactile, and kinesthetic learning? Visual learning styles include using pictures, videos, posters, flannel boards, puppets, and other eye-oriented treats. Auditory learning includes discussion, brief lecture, music, reading stories and Scripture, and dramatized recordings. Tactile learners prefer to touch objects and lock away learning with how things feel. Crafts offer great experiences to everyone, but especially to tactile learners! Kinesthetic learners are more physically active and learn best through lively games, devotions, skits, and such. Ignoring or using one learning style to the exclusion of others will lessen learning and not provide healthy balance. Look for lessons that offer variety!

SCRIPTURE. Doesn't it seem rather obvious that Christian programming would include Scripture? Most programs do at least *list* verses, but your new discerning eye will look for three important "Hows": HOW much Scripture is offered? HOW often is Scripture used in the lessons? HOW effectively is it taught or used?

Many children's resource products simply list verses as a basis for the activities, which is fine if the activities are brief and meant as only reinforcement or enrichment of themes. But in a curriculum you'll want Scripture at every turn! After all, this is the most intensive time you'll spend helping kids learn to know, love, and follow the Lord! Scripture needs to be taught, read, or alluded to in nearly every activity to be effective and to reinforce all that's being taught. Look for ways kids are encouraged to learn and apply God's Word in their lives. Do lessons encourage kids to repeat God's Word in lively, memorable ways? Is Scripture presented as the powerful, enjoyable, and relevant life tool it's meant to be? Examine your curriculum and other resources for the presence of Scripture, and be sure what you're teaching is as involved in God's Word as you want your kids to be!

Teacher Feature

ASSIMILATION. Think back to geometry or algebra classes you've taken. Unless you're a math major or statistician, you probably haven't used much if any of what you struggled to learn. No doubt those functions, graphing, and endless equations seemed pretty useless. Kids can begin to feel that way about Sunday school lessons as well if those lessons are not carefully taught, reinforced, and assimilated. Assimilated lessons give kids the chance to understand how and where their learning will help in real-life situations. Assimilation through review and recapping what's been learned will also help kids gather together the information and learning you've just imparted. Look for lessons and activities that concisely state a theme, then review that theme and end with a recap of what's been learned. Assimilation at the close of each lesson is one aspect that makes the Power Builders Curriculum Series so effective in helping kids retain and concisely gather together all they've learned.

CHALLENGES. What's more fun for kids than being challenged to go beyond the usual or ordinary? Most kids love challenges and rise to them with vigor and enthusiasm. Why not put this natural delight to work in learning? Lessons and activities that offer extra-time activities, challenges, or one-step-further activities encourage kids to continue the learning process. Extra-challenge Scripture verses to learn, Bible verses to look up, and service projects all offer kids healthy, success-oriented challenges. After all, how can you lose when going an extra mile for the Lord? If extra-time activities or take-home pages are offered, encourage kids to complete them with partners, at home, or over the next few weeks. And be sure to acknowledge the extra effort. Kids glow under praise for jobs well done, and it encourages them to try the next challenge with delight, confidence, and enthusiasm!

Goals, balance, Scripture, assimilation, and extra challenges are the five key ingredients for solid children's programming. Copy and snip out the checklist in the margin and carry it with you to bookstores or meetings to evaluate the resources you're choosing for children. No, kids aren't petunias, but the time you spend in cultivating, feeding, and readying the soil to plant the seeds of God's truth is the best gardening time you'll ever enjoy. Be choosy, look for quality, then watch the bounty of fruit your good choices help grow!

5 KEYS TO KIDS PROGRAMMING

- Are GOALS well stated and measurable?
- Is there BALANCE among the activities?
- What about SCRIPTURE? (How much, how often, how effective?)
- Is there ASSIMILATION, review, and recaps of learning?
- Does the curriculum offer extra CHALLENGES or take-home pages?

Parent Page

PARENT PAGE NEWSLETTER

Dear Parent:

Your child is about to embark on a wonderful exploration of the hope that we have in our faithful God! In the book *Hope Finders,* children will discover the three all-powerful sources of our hope, learn that Jesus' forgiveness and salvation promise us a hope and a future, explore ways to hold on to hope in hard times, discover that helping others gives us hope, explore ways to share our hope in Christ, learn the difference between everyday hopes and heavenly hope, plus much more. You can help in your child's learning process by:

★ joining in the fun of the take-home Power Pages,
★ discussing with your child how to find hope in "hopeless" situations,
★ helping your child learn the Mighty Memory Verses,
★ reading Bible verses on God's hope and sharing his hope with others,
★ portraying a positive role-model of faith and hope, and
★ inquiring how your child is doing on the Whiz Quiz reviews.

Being a part of your child's growing spiritual experience brings wonderful opportunities to share your own faith and love for God. God bless you as you discover the heavenly hope and assurance in being God's Hope Finders!

Then you will know that I am the LORD;
those who hope in me will not be disappointed.
Isaiah 49:23

Section 1

GOD'S GIFT OF HOPE

Be strong and take heart,
all you who hope in the LORD.
Psalm 31:24

Lesson 1

A PERFECT FOUNDATION

God sets hope before us through his promises.

Isaiah 40:31; 49:23
Jeremiah 14:22
Romans 15:4, 13

SESSION SUPPLIES

★ Bibles
★ masking tape & glue
★ white paper & newsprint
★ 6 medium-sized boxes
★ white shelf paper or brown wrapping paper
★ scissors, markers, glitter glue
★ 6-inch plastic plates
★ plaster or quick-set concrete
★ old coffee can and spoon
★ small pebbles or colored aquarium gravel
★ plastic jewels or large sequins
★ photocopies of the Words of Hope verses (page 15)
★ photocopies of the Power Page! (page 19)

MIGHTY MEMORY VERSE

Be strong and take heart, all you who hope in the LORD. Psalm 31:24

SESSION OBJECTIVES

During this session, children will
★ discover that hope springs from God
★ explore the foundation of hope God established for us
★ learn that hope never disappoints us
★ understand that hope is strengthened by faith

BIBLE BACKGROUND

Feelings of hopelessness or depression have become so prevalent in our modern world that the World Health Organization has listed depression or hopelessness as the most common affliction of all. Medical science has tried for years to come up with the perfect cure or treatment for hopelessness, but alas it seems a hopeless cause. Chemicals, situations, and other people don't hold the answer to finding hope in a hopeless world—but God does! In God, we have a perfect prescription for hope and help, love and everlasting life. And the cure is 100 percent effective, for Isaiah 49:23 tells us that those who hope in the Lord will not be disappointed!

Kids live in a fast-paced world often filled with frustrations, from broken homes and violence at school to negative peer pressure, all of which easily create feelings of hopelessness

Lesson 1

and withdrawal. It's important for kids to understand that hope from God is hope that lasts and never fails us. Use this lesson to help kids discover the heavenly foundation God has given us for hope, help, and happiness.

POWER FOCUS

Before class, collect rolls of masking tape and a sheet of white paper for every two kids.

Welcome kids warmly and let them know you're happy that they have come to class. Then invite kids to form pairs or trios and hand each small group a sheet of paper. Keep the masking tape next to groups, since they'll need to share the tape during this activity. Say: **I have a challenge for you today. Let's see if you and your partners can use paper and tape to make a base or foundation that's sturdy enough for a book to rest on. Your foundations must pass the 3-S test: Are they solid, strong, and steady? Work together and listen to each other's ideas, then make your foundations. You'll have five minutes to build.**

After five minutes, halt building of the foundations. Test each group's structure by placing a book or Bible on it and having kids assess the three S's. Is each foundation solid, strong, and steady? Then ask:

★ **Why is it important for foundations to be solid, strong, and steady?**
★ **What happens to things built on weak, wavering foundations?**

Say: **Foundations must be solid, strong, and steady, if they are to be of any use to build on. Our foundation of hope is the same way. Hope needs to be built on something strong, solid, and steady to give us comfort, confidence, and joyful expectations. Today and for the next several weeks, we'll be exploring hope—what it means to be hopeful and how hope helps us live each day with joy and the assurance of God's everlasting love. Today we'll discover how God gives us hope and how he purposely planned for our hope. We'll learn why God's promises give us hope and begin learning a new Mighty Memory Verse about the power of heavenly hope. Right now, let's discover the gems or jewels God gives us in his firm foundation of hope.**

THE MIGHTY MESSAGE

Before class, be sure you have six medium-sized boxes, all the same height or width. You'll be making a foundation of boxes against a wall, so the boxes

13

Lesson 1

need to be the same height across their tops. Cover the front of each box with white shelf paper or brown wrapping paper. (This will be the side of each box that shows when the foundation is made against a wall.) You'll need markers, glitter glue, and one photocopy of the Words of Hope verses from this activity. Cut the verse boxes apart.

Have partners join with others until you have six groups. Hand each group a box, markers, and a Words of Hope verse box. Explain that in this activity each group will read a verse, then decide which "jewel" or "gem" of hope the verse gives. In other words, kids will decide what God does, gives, or is that gives us hope. (For example, Hebrews 10:23 tells about God's kept promises, so promises would be a jewel in our foundation of hope.) You may wish to circulate and point out what jewels the verses hold. Here are the suggested jewels or gems of God's foundation of hope for each verse:

★ Psalm 25:5—a foundation of TRUTH
★ Romans 15:4—a foundation of ENDURANCE or ENCOURAGEMENT
★ Hebrews 10:23—a foundation of KEPT PROMISES
★ Isaiah 40:31—a foundation of STRENGTH
★ Isaiah 49:23c—a foundation of FAITH or ASSURANCE
★ Jeremiah 14:22—a foundation of GOD'S CONTROL

Have groups write the jewel from their own verses on the fronts of the boxes. Then use glitter glue to draw a large gem shape or circle around the word. Finally, have kids glue their Words of Hope verses to the fronts of the boxes.

Have each group read its verse aloud for the entire class, then discuss what the jewel in God's foundation of hope is and why. After each is read, set that box against the wall as you build a foundation in a 3-2-1 pattern.

When all the verses have been read, ask:

★ **How does God's truth help us have hope?**
★ **In what ways does knowing that God is in control give us hope?**
★ **Could we have hope if God never kept his promises? Why not?**
★ **What are things we hope for in God?** (love, help, peace, understanding, forgiveness, guidance)
★ **How do faith and trust strengthen our hope that God will help us?**

POWER POINTERS

Make a list of times kids have felt hopeless or discouraged. Turn the list into a psalm by repeating "But in God I have heavenly hope" after each item is read.

Lesson 1

Say: **We live in a world where it's hard to have hope at times. We read about fights and arguments and mean-hearted people and know that good people can get hurt. Sometimes we become frustrated and feel hopeless. But God is smart, and he knew we would feel discouraged and hopeless at times, so he planned to give us special hope. God laid a foundation of heavenly hope for us through gifts he has given. We'll call these gifts "jewels" or "gems." It's important to know that God is always here offering us the hope we need through his jewels of . . .** (read aloud the jewels of God's foundation of hope on the fronts of the boxes).

It's also important to remember that we're never without hope when we know, love, and follow God. We just need to look for those precious jewels in times that feel frustrating or hopeless. Now let's make cool Hope Stones to remind us of the foundation of hope God has planned for and given us.

WORDS OF HOPE VERSES

"Guide me in your truth and teach me, for you are God my Savior, and my hope is in you all day long." *Psalm 25:5*

"For everything that was written in the past was written to teach us, so that through endurance and the encouragement of the Scriptures we might have hope." *Romans 15:4*

"Let us hold unswervingly to the hope we profess, for he who promised is faithful." *Hebrews 10:23*

"But those who hope in the LORD will renew their strength. They will soar on wings like eagles; they will run and not grow weary, they will walk and not be faint." *Isaiah 40:31*

"Then you will know that I am the LORD; those who hope in me will not be disappointed." *Isaiah 49:23c*

"Do any of the worthless idols of the nations bring rain? Do the skies themselves send down showers? No, it is you, O LORD our God. Therefore our hope is in you, for you are the one who does all this." *Jeremiah 14:22*

Lesson 1

THE MESSAGE IN MOTION

Before class, you'll need to collect 6-inch plastic plates, small pebbles or colored aquarium gravel, and plastic jewels or large sequins. You'll also need to mix plaster of Paris or quick-set concrete to pour in the plates. Mix the plaster or concrete in an empty coffee can according to the package directions, stirring with an old spoon. (You may use self-hardening clay.) Mix the plaster or concrete just prior to this activity.

Hand each child a plastic plate and explain that you'll be making Hope Stones that are made of strong, sturdy materials to remind kids of the strong foundation of hope God has given us. Point out that kids will be using small pebbles or aquarium gravel to form the words "Hope in" and plastic jewels or large sequins to form the word "God!"

Pour quick-set concrete or plaster into the plastic plates so there's ½-inch of thick material on the plate. (If you're using self-hardening clay, have kids pat out a 5-by-½-inch thick circle on their plates.) Show kids how to carefully poke the small pebbles and colored aquarium gravel into the hardening plaster or concrete to form the words "Hope" and "in." (Don't push the pebbles in too deeply.) Then use plastic jewels or large sequins to form the word "God" The plaster or concrete will solidify in about ten minutes but must set overnight to be completely hardened (as does the clay). Let kids take their Hope Stones home on the plastic plates. Tell kids that they can simply "pop" their stones carefully out of the plastic in twenty-four hours.

Say: **Your Hope Stones are beautiful reminders of God's foundation of hope and how we're to trust in that strong foundation. Place your Hope Stones on a desk or table, and each time you see it, remember to thank God for the hope of love, help, and forgiveness he freely offers us each day.**

One of the verses we read earlier tells us that Scripture or God's Word gives us encouragement and hope. Let's discover hope through learning God's Word in our new Mighty Memory Verse.

SUPER SCRIPTURE

Before class, draw the rebus pictures for Psalm 31:24 (see margin) on a sheet of newsprint. Tape the verse in a place where kids can see and read it.

Gather kids by the rebus verse and repeat Psalm 31:24 three times as you point to the pictures. Then say: **What an important verse to keep in mind as we seek hope in the Lord! Psalm 31:24 tells us to do two things: we must be strong, and we must take heart or be encouraged. In other words, this verse teaches us that we'll find hope if we trust and have faith in God.** Ask:

★ **If hope comes from God, how can it help us to trust and have faith in God?**

★ **How can we trust in God even more?**

Say: **When we read the Bible, learn God's Word, obey God, and love him, we strengthen our trust and faith. And when we have a strong foundation of trust and faith, we have heavenly hope that can never be taken away! God himself said, "Those who hope in me will not be disappointed"** (Isaiah 49:23c). **Wow! If we put our hope in God and his power, we'll never be disappointed. That not only gives me hope; it gives me joy, encouragement, and a wonderful promise right from God! You know, having hope feels so great, it also makes me want to thank God for giving us hope. Let's share a prayer thanking God for giving us such a perfect foundation of heavenly hope.** Keep the newsprint rebus verse to use next week.

A POWERFUL PROMISE

Have kids sit in a circle holding their Hope Stones on the plates. Say: **We've been learning today about God's plan for and perfect foundation of hope. We've learned that God gives us hope through truth, faithfulness, promises, love, forgiveness, and strength. And we began learning**

Lesson 1

a new Mighty Memory Verse that teaches us to be strong and take heart. Psalm 31:24 says (encourage kids to repeat the verse with you), "Be strong and take heart, all you who hope in the LORD."

Say: **Let's go around the circle and offer God a prayer of thanks for giving us hope. When it's your turn, place your Hope Stone in the center of the circle and say, "Thank you, God, for hope through…," then name one of the jewels from our boxes. I'll go first to show you. Dear Lord, thank you for hope through your kept promises.**

When all the Hope Stones are in the center of the circle, have kids join hands and end with a corporate "amen." Say: **God's hope is always here for us and will never disappoint us or be taken away.** Read aloud Romans 15:13, then end with this responsive good-bye:

Leader: **May God's hope be with you.**

Children: **And also with you!**

Distribute the Power Page! take-home papers as kids are leaving and remind them to take home their Hope Stones. Thank children for coming and encourage them to seek God's jewels of hope this week.

Lesson 1   **God's Gift of Hope**

POWER PAGE!

LAYING A FOUNDATION OF HOPE

Crack the code to discover how God lays a perfect foundation of hope in our lives.

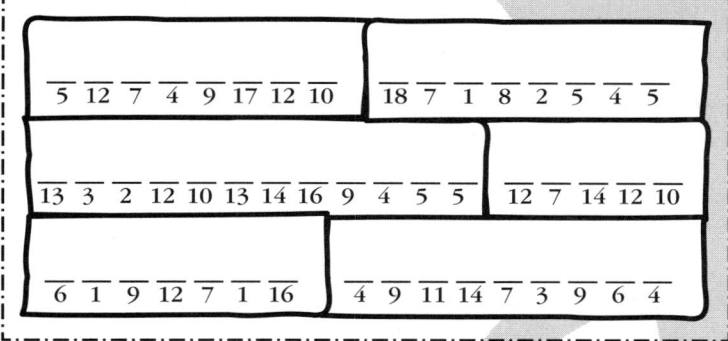

A = 3
C = 6
D = 11
E = 4
F = 13
G = 17
H = 10
I = 2
K = 19
L = 16

M = 8
N = 9
O = 1
P = 18
R = 7
S = 5
T = 12
U = 14
V = 15

5 12 7 4 9 17 12 10   18 7 1 8 2 5 4 5

13 3 2 12 10 13 14 16 9 4 5 5   12 7 14 12 10

6 1 9 12 7 1 16   4 9 11 14 7 3 9 6 4

Try This!

Find a fluffy feather and tie thread to the end. Hold your feather a few inches above a light bulb. (Turn on the lamp and remove the lampshade.) After a few moments, your feather will lift and move! Neat, isn't it? **God** lifts us with hope in the same way! He renews our strength, and we can soar like a certain kind of bird.

Unscramble this word to discover what bird Isaiah 40:31 mentions!

LEGAE

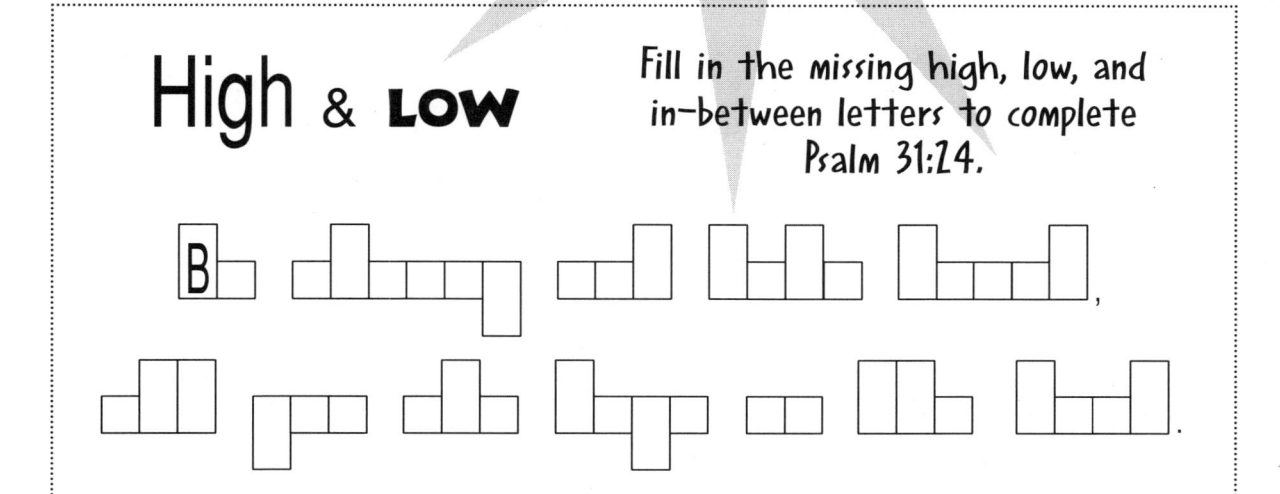

_____

High & Low

Fill in the missing high, low, and in-between letters to complete Psalm 31:24.

B _ ,

_ .

© 2001 by Susan L. Lingo.
Permission is granted to reproduce this page for ministry purposes only—not for resale.

19

Lesson 2

A HEAVENLY HOPE

God gave us hope through sending Jesus to love us!

Isaiah 42:1-4
Luke 2:4-14
1 Peter 1:3

SESSION SUPPLIES

- ★ Bibles
- ★ newsprint & tape
- ★ markers & scissors
- ★ construction paper & glue
- ★ white satin ribbon
- ★ paper plates, plastic spoons, & a knife
- ★ pound cake & frozen strawberries
- ★ star-shaped cookie cutters
- ★ whipped topping & green candy sprinkles
- ★ photocopies of the Christmas Star patterns (page 123)
- ★ photocopies of the Power Page! (page 27)

MIGHTY MEMORY VERSE

Be strong and take heart, all you who hope in the LORD. Psalm 31:24

(For older kids, add in Micah 7:7: "But as for me, I watch in hope for the LORD, I wait for God my Savior; my God will hear me.")

SESSION OBJECTIVES

During this session, children will
★ discover that God had a plan for our hope
★ learn that Jesus was God's plan for salvation
★ understand that Jesus gives us hope
★ express thanks for Jesus, who is our living hope

BIBLE BACKGROUND

Think for a moment of things you consider a *need*. Some of us might mention televisions, e-mail to stay in touch, or even cell phones to check in with the family. Others might consider more basic necessities such as clothing, food, and housing. But can any need, real or perceived, compare with our need for hope and the forgiveness of sin? Though we may be pretty good at supplying for our own earthly needs, God alone provides for our spiritual needs of forgiveness and hope. It was a plan God promised from the beginning of time (Titus 1:2) and then began to fulfill with the joyous birth of Jesus.

Of course kids find joy, excitement, and fun in the celebration of Christmas, but they don't often stop to consider the hope this special season brings. Help kids understand that Christmas and the celebration of Jesus' birth come from God's perfect plan for our hope. Use this lesson in December or anytime you want kids to feel the joy of hope fulfilled through Christ.

POWER FOCUS

Before class, write the following directions on newsprint. Tape the newsprint to a wall where kids can read the directions.
1. Choose a sheet of construction paper.
2. Draw a large star on the paper.
3. Cut out the star.
4. Put your name on the back.

Welcome kids and let them know you're glad they're in class. Then have kids sit in a group by the newsprint directions. Say: **For our time today, we need some nice, large paper stars. You know, anytime we need something there must be a plan to provide for those needs. I have a plan here on newsprint. Who can read the plan aloud?** Choose a volunteer to read aloud the directions, then have the kids follow the plan to make large paper stars.

When everyone has cut out a paper star, say: **You followed the plan, and see what it accomplished? You all have the nice, big stars we need for today. Did you know that God knows every one of our needs? God knows we need love, forgiveness, teaching, guidance, and salvation to keep us happy and on the right track. In other words, God knows we need hope in our lives, so long ago God planned for our hope by sending us a special gift. Today we'll discover how God planned for us to have hope. We'll also learn that through Jesus we can have hope, help, and happiness. And we'll review the Mighty Memory Verse that we began learning last week. Right now, we can use our paper stars to discover how God planned for and provided us with joyous hope!**

THE MIGHTY MESSAGE

Before class, make a photocopy of the Christmas patterns from page 123 for each child. If possible, use stiff paper to make the copies. Cut a 10-inch

Lesson 2

length of white satin ribbon for each child. You'll also need markers, scissors, and glue.

Have kids hold the paper stars they just made, then distribute copies of the Christmas-story patterns. Say: **The stars you made in the last activity remind me of the night Jesus was born. On that starry night, joyous hope entered the sad world according to God's plan. There are five points on the stars, so we'll read five verses and discover five important ways God has given us hope through the wondrous birth of his Son, Jesus! Let's do the top star point first.** Read aloud Isaiah 42:1-4, then ask:

★ Why did nations, or the world long ago, need hope?

★ Why do we need hope in our world today?

Say: **God knew the world was filled with sin and hopelessness. After all, how could we be forgiven for all the sin in the world? Well, God knew we needed a plan for hope, so he promised to send the world a Savior, one who would forgive us and love us and bring us hope for a bright future. God gave us hope through his promise!** Have kids cut out and glue the star patterns to the top points of their stars, then write "promise" on the back of the points. Color the stars yellow.

Read aloud Psalm 119:41, then say: **People believed in God's promise and began to hope for and expect a Savior.** Glue the patterns for the two people on the two points just below the star to show how people began to have hope that a Savior would come. Then write the word "hope" on the back of one of those points and the word "expect" on the other.

Color the people patterns.

Read aloud Luke 2:10, 11. Then ask:

★ Why is Jesus a great joy for all people?

★ How did Jesus' birth bring us a living hope?

POWER POINTERS

Host a Hope Drive to give needy kids and families a bit of Christmas joy. Collect gently used books and storybooks to distribute to a homeless shelter or local family agency.

Say: **When Jesus was born that starry night, a living hope came into the world! God had fulfilled his promise of a Savior. God gave us hope through fulfilling his greatest promise!** Have kids glue the manger and baby Jesus to the centers of their stars and write the word "fulfillment" on the center backs of the stars.

Read aloud Titus 1:2, then say: **God *promised* us the hope of eternal life, and he *accomplished* that promise through Jesus' birth and death on the cross. Through Jesus' loving forgiveness, we have the assurance of eternal life!** Glue the cross shapes to the lower right points of the stars and write the word "forgiveness" on the backs of those points.

Finally, read aloud 1 Peter 1:3, then say: **God has given us hope through the great joy we experience when we know we can have new life in Jesus.** Glue the heart shapes, which stand for love and joy, to the last point on your stars. Then write the word "joy" on the back of that point.

When the stars are done, say: **Wasn't God's plan for our hope perfect? Turn your stars over so you can read the words.** Have kids point to the words on the star as each is mentioned. **See how God has given us hope through his *promise*, which brought people great *hope?* God fulfilled his promise by sending *Jesus*, who brought us *forgiveness* and who gives us the *joy* and hope of eternal life. Now turn your star over. You have the whole Christmas story on your star! The star above is baby Jesus. Mary and Joseph are nearby, and love, forgiveness, and joy are surrounding them! Let's put hangers on your Christmas-story stars to make ornaments that remind us of God's perfect plan for hope. Then you can share with your families and friends the story of Christmas and how God brought hope into the world through Jesus' birth.** Glue or tape the white ribbons to the tops of the stars to make ornaments.

THE MESSAGE IN MOTION

Before class, gather star-shaped cookie cutters, pound cake, a knife, paper plates, whipped topping, frozen strawberries, plastic spoons, and green candy sprinkles. Be sure that when the pound cake is sliced into ½-inch-thick slices, kids will be able to cut star shapes from the cake. You may wish to slice the cake ahead of time.

Set the ingredients, paper plates, and plastic spoons on a table. Say: **Celebrating Jesus' birth and the hope of love, forgiveness, and eternal**

Lesson 2

life that he brings us brings such joy! Let's celebrate now with a special holiday treat as we review God's plan for our hope.

Hand each child a plate and say: **You're holding empty plates, but you know a special treat is coming. You have the promise of something wonderful. God promised something wonderful when he promised a Savior for the world. And as you look over these delicious ingredients, you have the hope of a tasty treat.** Give each child a slice of pound cake, then let kids use the cookie cutters to cut star shapes in the cake. Spoon strawberries over the stars and add a dollop of whipped topping to each. Finally, let kids shake green candy sprinkles over their treats.

When the goodies are prepared, say: **Wow! Your treats are yummy looking, and the promise of something good to eat has been fulfilled. When Jesus was born to us, God fulfilled his plan to send us the promised Savior. You have the assurance of a sweet treat, and we have assurance of sweet love and hope through Jesus!**

As kids are eating their snacks, say: **Mmm, our treats are wonderful, and I can see you're enjoying them greatly. We have joy from the hope Jesus brings us too! God's perfect plan for hope included his promise, the birth of Jesus as our living hope, the assurance of salvation through Jesus, and the joy God's plan brings us. We also have hope through God's Word. Let's review our Mighty Memory Verse as we learn more about the hope that comes from Jesus.**

SUPER SCRIPTURE

Be sure you have the rebus verse written on newsprint from last week. Tape the verse to the wall or door for kids to see.

Repeat Psalm 31:24 two times aloud, then ask for volunteers who would like to repeat the verse aloud. Hold up a star and say: **We can use our story stars to help us**

Lesson 2

repeat the Mighty Memory Verse like this: **Be strong** (point to the star) **and take heart** (point to the heart), **all you** (point to the figures of the people) **who hope** (point to the cross) **in the Lord** (point to the figure of Jesus).

Lead kids in repeating Psalm 31:24 as they point to the points of their story stars. (If you have older kids, introduce Micah 7:7 at this time.)

Say: **God had a perfect plan to give us a future and a hope, and he sent Jesus to us as part of that heavenly plan.** Ask:

★ **In what ways is hope through Jesus a perfect hope?**

★ **How does hope through Jesus make us strong? help us take heart?**

Say: **Jesus is our living hope and the fulfillment of God's promise to us of salvation, love, forgiveness, and eternal life. No wonder Jesus brings us such awesome joy! Let's share a prayer thanking God for planning for our hope and for sending Jesus to be our living hope.** Save the rebus verse on newsprint to use next week.

A POWERFUL PROMISE

Have kids sit in a circle holding their story-star ornaments. Say: **We've been learning today that God had a perfect plan to bring us hope. We discovered that Jesus was sent to us as a living hope. And we reviewed the Mighty Memory Verse that says** (encourage kids to repeat Psalm 31:24), **Be strong and take heart, all you who hope in the Lord.** (Repeat Micah 7:7 with older kids.)

Say: **Let's offer a prayer to God thanking him for his plan for hope and for bringing us hope through Jesus. Then we'll end by going around the circle as you thank God by reading one of the ways he brings hope from the back of your star.** For example, you can say, "Thank you for giving me hope through the gift of Jesus, Lord." Pray: **Dear Lord, thank you for knowing our needs and for knowing we need hope.**

25

Lesson 2

We're so thankful for your plan for hope through Jesus and his loving forgiveness. Amen. Continue around the circle until everyone has had a turn to thank God using the story stars.

End with this responsive good-bye:

Leader: **May the hope of Jesus be with you.**

Children: **And also with you!**

Distribute the Power Page! take-home papers as kids are leaving. Thank children for coming and encourage them to share the story on their Christmas-story stars with their families and friends to remind them of God's perfect plan for hope through Jesus.

Lesson 2 — **God's Gift of Hope**

POWER PAGE!

Points of Hope!

See if you can find each point of hope Jesus brings to us. Look up the verses and write the words in the spaces.

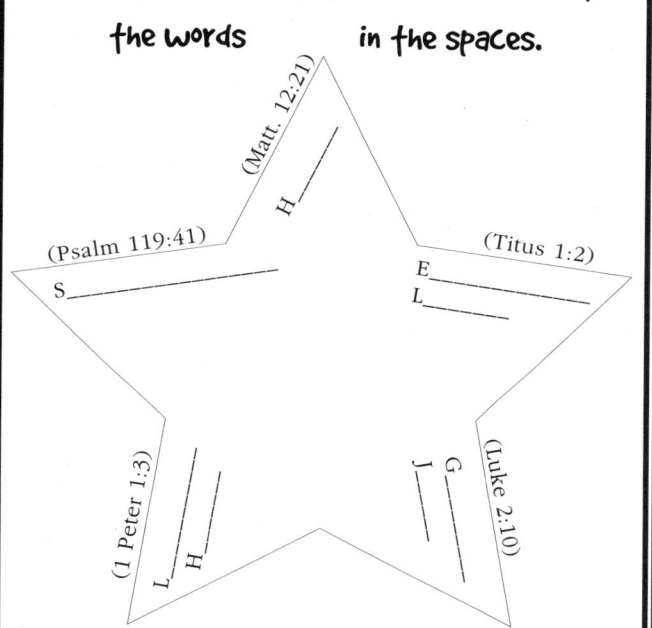

- (Matt. 12:21) H____
- (Psalm 119:41) S____
- (Titus 1:2) E____ L____
- (1 Peter 1:3) L____ H____
- (Luke 2:10) G____ J____

Christmas Craft

Make this cute ornament to hang on your Christmas tree to remind you that Jesus came as our living hope!

You'll need:
- ★ an ice-cream cone
- ★ straw or dried grass
- ★ satin Christmas ball
- ★ paper star
- ★ ribbon
- ★ markers
- ★ tacky glue

Directions:
1. Glue straw or dried grass around the edge of the cone.
2. Glue the Christmas ball to the cone.
3. Draw a face to the Christmas ball.
4. Glue a 10-inch length of ribbon to to the cone as a hanger.
5. Glue a paper star on the ribbon above baby Jesus.

Crazy Circuit Board

Follow the arrows to plug in the missing letters from Psalm 31:24.

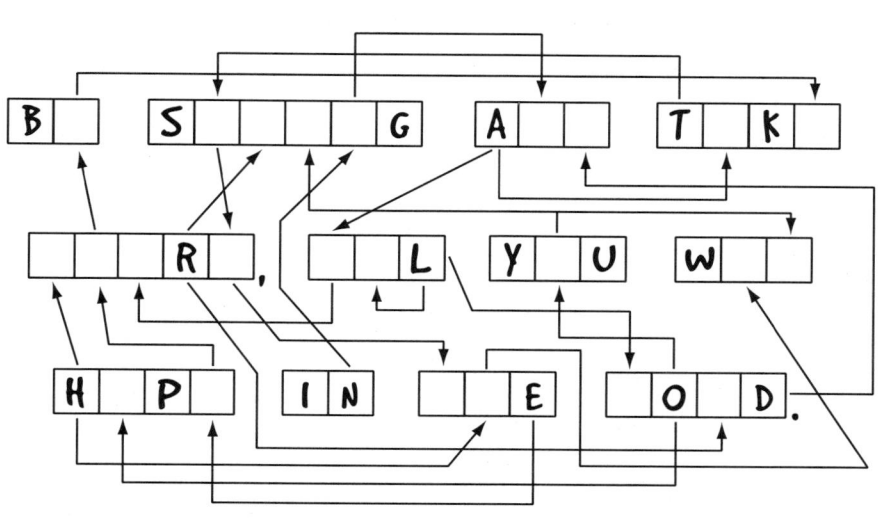

B_ S__ G A_ T_ K
_ R_, _ L_ Y U W_
H_ P _ IN _ E _ O D.

© 2001 by Susan L. Lingo.
Permission is granted to reproduce this page for ministry purposes only—not for resale.

Lesson 3

A SPIRIT OF HOPE

The Holy Spirit helps us recognize hope in our lives.

Romans 8:9, 14, 16
1 Corinthians 2:12
Galatians 5:5
Ephesians 4:4-6

SESSION SUPPLIES

★ Bibles
★ white paper & construction paper
★ markers & scissors
★ shaving cream or lathery soap
★ window cleaner & paper towels
★ black stained-glass squeeze paint
★ 8½-by-11-inch picture frames (see Power Focus)
★ balloons
★ photocopies of the Whiz Quiz (page 36) and the Power Page! (page 35)

MIGHTY MEMORY VERSE

Be strong and take heart, all you who hope in the LORD. Psalm 31:24

(For older kids, add in Micah 7:7: "But as for me, I watch in hope for the LORD, I wait for God my Savior; my God will hear me.")

SESSION OBJECTIVES

During this session, children will
★ learn that the Holy Spirit brings us hope
★ discover how the Holy Spirit helps us "hang on"
★ understand that the Spirit helps us recognize God's blessings
★ know there is one Spirit, one Lord, and one hope

BIBLE BACKGROUND

You know the famous test for pessimism versus optimism. If you look at a half-filled glass, what do you see: a glass half empty or one half full? All too often we tend to look at life as a half-empty glass. We see the trouble spots, feel the bumps and bruises of hurt and shattered dreams, and keep score when things don't go our way. To see a glass half empty is to ignore hope and to discount the blessings God freely gives us. That's where the Holy Spirit steps in! The Spirit of God helps us recognize and remember all the blessings, promises, gifts, grace, and hope that God showers on us. And as the Spirit pours his love and power into our hearts, that glass suddenly becomes full and overflows with hope and happiness!

Kids especially need reminders of God's grace and blessings, since even one hard day or a fleeting hopeless feeling can seem like the end of the world and last forever. Kids have trouble understanding that trying situations can and do get better and that even in the midst of sadness and hopelessness, God showers his blessings on us. We simply need to take the time to look for them. Use this lesson to teach kids that the Holy Spirit will give them hope as he helps them recognize and remember God's gifts in their lives.

POWER Focus

Before class, you'll need to purchase an inexpensive 8½-by-11-inch picture frame with glass for each child, plus one extra. (Smaller frames will work but won't be as nice.) You'll be turning these inexpensive frames into "Windows of Hope" throughout this lesson. Write "The Holy Spirit's Window of Hope" on a sheet of white copy paper. Slide the paper into one of the 8½-by-11-inch frames, under the glass. Smudge the glass with a bit of shaving cream or lathery soap to cloud the glass and blur the words. Kids will use window cleaner to clean off the haze.

Welcome kids and invite them to sit in a group. Ask kids if they've ever looked through a smudgy or cloudy window. Invite several volunteers to tell what it was like to have their vision blurred or blocked. After kids share their experiences, hold up the picture frame with the blurry glass. Say: **Sometimes we find ourselves looking through a haze or not being able to see difficult situations clearly.** Ask:

★ **How is looking through a hazy window like feeling hopeless?**

★ **In what ways does feeling hopeless and helpless block our vision of happiness? of God?**

Say: **Hopelessness is like looking through a smudgy window. It makes us unable to see the bright blessings in our lives or forget God's goodness and grace. We need a special window cleaner to restore our sight!** Let kids use paper towels and the window cleaner to clean the window. Then say: **Spray window cleaner works well on glass. See how much easier it is to look through our "window"? What does the paper in the window say?** Invite a volunteer to read the paper, then continue: **The Holy Spirit can clean away our hopelessness and help us**

Lesson 3

see hope more clearly—just as the window cleaner helped us see God's truth more clearly. You might say that the Holy Spirit gives us a clear window of hope!

Today we'll learn how the Holy Spirit helps us see God's blessings and hang on to hope when things seem cloudy and hopeless. We'll also review our Mighty Memory Verse, which teaches us about where hope comes from. First, let's use pretend windows as we discover more about the Holy Spirit's Window of Hope by reading some powerful Bible verses.

THE MIGHTY MESSAGE

Before class, collect black squeeze paint, white paper, and colorful markers. Kids will use markers to draw scenes on white paper, then insert the scenes into picture frames as pretend windows. They'll finish by using stained-glass squeeze paint to add window-pane lines to the glass.

Hand each child a sheet of white paper and a picture frame. Say: **Let's pretend these frames are really beautiful windows. But they're so empty right now—they need beautiful scenes to look out on! We'll read a few verses as we learn more about how the Holy Spirit helps us have hope. As we read, we'll draw a scene to go in our windows and give us a beautiful reminder of the hope we find through God's Spirit.**

POWER POINTERS

Kids might enjoy cleaning windows in the church or hosting a car-window cleaning service. After windows sparkle, leave notes saying, "Let hope shine through!"

Read aloud 1 Corinthians 2:12. Then say: **The Holy Spirit gives us hope by helping us recognize God's blessings, which include Jesus. What other blessings has God given you?** Allow time for responses, then continue: **When we feel hopeless, it's almost like having a cloudy day. But we know the clouds will go away in time—and the Holy Spirit helps us remember God's blessings in the meantime. Use markers to draw fluffy clouds and a peeking sun in your scene to remind us how the Spirit clears away the clouds so we can recognize and remember all God has given us.**

Read aloud Galatians 5:5, then say: **It often takes great patience and perseverance to wait for those clouds in our lives to clear, doesn't it?**

But the Holy Spirit brings us hope through patience and helping us be strong. Draw a big, strong tree in your scene to remind us how hope often takes strength and patience. (Tell kids to leave blank circles on their trees, since they will draw apples in a moment.)

Read aloud Romans 8:9, 14, and 16. Then say: **When we're led by the Spirit, we live with the hope of Jesus and know his forgiving love will help us. The Holy Spirit leads us and keeps us strong in Jesus so we can produce good fruit in our lives, such as helping others, serving God, and speaking kind words. Draw apples on your tree to remind you that the Spirit helps us produce the good fruit that Jesus wants us to have in our lives.**

Read aloud Ephesians 4:4-6. Say: **We know there is one God, one faith, one Lord, and one baptism in Jesus. But there is also one Spirit and one hope. The Holy Spirit reminds us that we are called to hope in our one God, who is God over all! Draw one huge mountain in your scene to remind you of the power of our one God and one hope in our lives!**

When the pictures are complete, ask:

★ How does having patience help us hang on to hope?
★ How can being led by God's Spirit lead us to hope? to trust in God?
★ In what ways does living as Jesus wants help us have hope?

Say: **The Holy Spirit brings us hope by clearing away the clouds of doubt and hopelessness, and he reminds us of God's blessings when we sometimes forget them. What a wonderful window of hope the Spirit gives!**

Have kids put their scenes into the plastic picture-frame "windows," then use black stained-glass squeeze paint to divide the windows and make four panes on the glass.

Say: **When your windows dry, hang them in your room to remind you that the Holy Spirit gives you a special window of hope to clearly see God's blessings in your life in even the cloudiest of times! Now let's play a lively game to remind us how the Holy Spirit helps us break through things that may keep us from having hope.**

Lesson 3

THE MESSAGE IN MOTION

Before class, cut out a 3-inch construction-paper heart for each child and write the words "Hope from the Spirit" on each heart. Fold the hearts into small rectangles and push them through the necks of balloons so they fall inside the uninflated balloons. Prepare a balloon for each child.

Have kids form two or three lines at one end of the room. Place the uninflated balloons at the opposite end of the room. Explain that this is a two-part relay race. For the first part, kids must hop to collect a balloon, then hop and return to their lines so the next person can go. When all the members of one line have balloons, give each other high fives, then sit down.

When everyone has a balloon, have kids blow up and tie off the balloons. Then say: **Shake your balloons. Do you feel something inside? That's hope, but we can't get to it because the balloon is blocking us. What are things that often keep us from having hope?** Lead kids to tell that doubt, sadness, angry feelings, lack of faith, discouragement, and even being hungry or tired can keep us from having hope.

Say: **Did you know that Satan doesn't want us to have hope? That's right! Satan knows that hope keeps us close to God, and that makes him mad. He wants us to be separated from hope. But the power of the Holy Spirit helps us break through the obstacles to find hope! In the next part of this race, you must break through to find your hope by popping your balloon by standing or sitting on it. When you've broken through to find your hope, shout, "The Spirit helps us have hope!"**

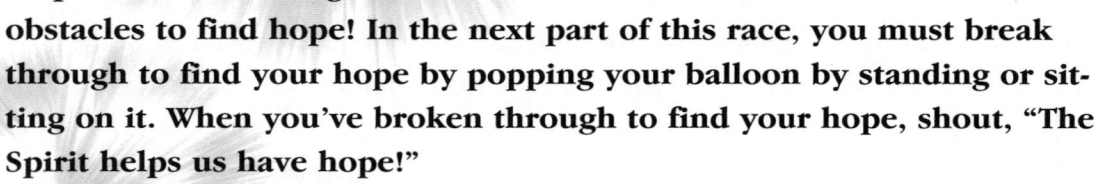

After kids have opened their paper hearts, say: **The Holy Spirit's power helps us in so many ways to find hope. One way is through helping us learn God's Word. Let's review our Mighty Memory Verse as we discover more about having hope.**

Lesson 3

SUPER SCRIPTURE

Before this activity, cut the rebus verse on newsprint into as many pieces as you have kids. If you have more than fifteen kids, make two puzzles. (If you have older kids who began learning Micah 7:7 last week, make a puzzle for that verse too.)

Repeat Psalm 34:21 two times aloud, then hand each child a puzzle piece. When you say, "Go," see how quickly kids can work together to reassemble the verse. When the verse is complete, read it aloud in unison. Then ask:

★ **What can you do to be strong in God when feelings of hopelessness creep up?**

★ **In what ways can the Holy Spirit help us be strong and take heart?**

★ **How can reminding ourselves of God's blessings help us be strong and take heart?**

Say: **I'm so glad that the Holy Spirit helps me recognize God's blessings when I start feeling sad, doubtful, or hopeless. Sometimes I forget all that God has freely given me, and I need the Holy Spirit to remind me. Then I discover I have strong faith and hope and find myself smiling again! Let's thank the Holy Spirit for helping us have a spirit of hope.**

A POWERFUL PROMISE

Have kids lean their Windows of Hope scenes against the wall and sit a few feet away from them with their eyes closed. Quietly say: **Sometimes we forget where our hope lies. We can't see anything but darkness and sadness, and we begin to feel hopeless. But the Holy Spirit is here to remind us that he will help open our eyes to hope.** Have kids open their eyes and look at the scenes in front of them. **We've learned today that God's Spirit helps us recognize and remember all the blessings God freely gives us. We've discovered that being led by the Spirit brings us hope through living as Jesus desires. And we've reviewed our Mighty Memory Verse that says, "Be strong and take heart, all you who hope in the LORD."** (Repeat Micah 7:7 with older kids.)

Hold up the Bible and say: **God's Word is filled with the blessings God gives us, all of which bring us hope. It's up to us to remember those blessings in times of doubt—and the Holy Spirit will help us do that.**

Lesson 3

Let's pass the Bible to each other. When it's your turn to hold the Bible, say, "Lord, please help me always remember your blessings."

When everyone has had a turn to hold the Bible, close with a prayer thanking the Holy Spirit for his help in giving us hope.

Before kids leave, allow five or ten minutes to complete the Whiz Quiz from page 36. If you run out of time, be sure to complete this page first thing next week. The Whiz Quiz is an invaluable tool that allows kids, teachers, and parents see what kids have learned in the previous three weeks.

End with this responsive good-bye:

Leader: **May the Holy Spirit's hope be with you.**

Children: **And also with you!**

Distribute the Power Page! take-home papers as kids are leaving. Thank children for coming and remind them to take home their Windows of Hope.

Lesson 3 **God's Gift of Hope**

POWER PAGE!

SCRIPTURE SAFARI

Read the verses and draw lines to how the Holy Spirit gives us hope.

Recognize what God freely gives us.   Gal. 5:5

Gives us patience so we can wait with hope.   Eph. 4:4-6

Leads us so we can be sons of God.   1 Cor. 2:12

Reminds us of one hope, one Lord, & one God over all.   Rom. 8:14

Blessing Bits

Make simple & scrumptious reminders of God's blessings to share with your family!

Whatcha need:
- ★ folded-over potato chips
- ★ melted choloate chips
- ★ small slips of paper
- ★ spoon
- ★ waxed paper
- ★ pen or pencil

Whatcha do:
1. Write a blessing on each slip of paper (family, love, hope, truth, flowers, etc.).
2. Slide one slip into a folded-over chip.
3. Put the chips on waxed paper and drizzle melted chocolate over them.
4. Put chips in a cool place until the chocolate hardens.
5. Break open the chips and read the blessings with your family!

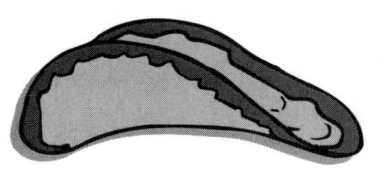

Seek-n-Search

Find the words to Psalm 34:21 in the puzzle box, then write the words in the spaces below.

__ _____ ___

____ _____, ___

___ ___ ____

__ ___ ____.

Q	M	T	H	E	P	A	N	D
D	L	R	S	H	A	B	C	F
W	O	X	Y	E	L	E	X	H
I	R	B	C	A	L	Y	N	O
S	D	S	T	R	O	N	G	P
W	R	N	P	T	N	E	Y	E
H	D	T	A	K	E	X	Z	L
O	A	Y	O	U	I	N	S	R

© 2001 by Susan L. Lingo.
Permission is granted to reproduce this page for ministry purposes only—not for resale.

Section I   **God's Gift of Hope**

WHIZ QUIZ

Color in T (true) or F (false) to answer the questions.

➤ God gives us hope through his promises.   T F

➤ God didn't plan for our hope.   T F

➤ Jesus is our living hope.   T F

➤ We have hope through salvation.   T F

➤ The Holy Spirit wants us to lead ourselves.   T F

➤ The Holy Spirit reminds us of God's blessings.   T F

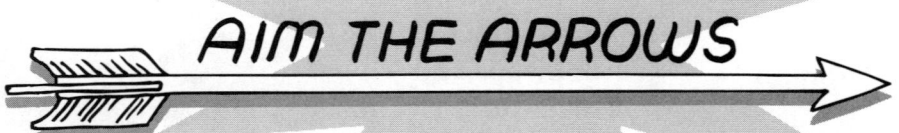

AIM THE ARROWS

Draw arrows to place the words in their correct positions to complete the Mighty Memory Verse. The first word has been done for you.

Words: strong, heart, take, all, and, who, Be, Be, in, you, the, Lord, 21, hope, 34, Psalm

Be ___ ___ ___ ___ ___ ___ ___,

___ ___ ___ ___ ___ ___,

___ ___ ___ ___ ___ ___ ___ ___,

___ ___ ___ ___ ___.

© 2001 by Susan L. Lingo.
Permission is granted to reproduce this page for ministry purposes only—not for resale.

Section 2

HOPE FOR TOMORROW

There is surely a future hope for you, and your hope will not be cut off.
Proverbs 23:18

Lesson 4

FAITH IN THE FUTURE

God has promised us a future hope.

Psalms 33:11; 131:3
Jeremiah 29:11
Ephesians 2:10

SESSION SUPPLIES

★ Bibles
★ poster board
★ markers & scissors
★ a colorful magazine picture
★ tape & tacky craft glue
★ red cellophane paper
★ dry ice (see Mighty Message)
★ cooking pot
★ roll of white shelf paper
★ white ribbon
★ red & blue crayons
★ photocopies of the Future Cards (page 124)
★ photocopies of the Cool Shades pattern (page 124)
★ photocopies of the Power Page! (page 45)

MIGHTY MEMORY VERSE

There is surely a future hope for you, and your hope will not be cut off. Proverbs 23:18

SESSION OBJECTIVES

During this session, children will
★ discover that God promised us a hope and a future
★ learn that hope and the future are connected
★ explore what our future holds with God
★ realize that our hope and future cannot be taken away

BIBLE BACKGROUND

It seems as though we're always being told to plan for our futures. But usually the focus is on finances, such as planning for retirement, estate planning, or even planning for our kids' college education. Planning for the future can be difficult, since we don't know what to expect. But the future holds so much more than earthly retirement homes or estate planning—it holds an eternal hope for a heavenly home that can't be purchased with retirement funds. Isn't it great that our heavenly estate planner is already at work planning a future hope and home for us? And God has been planning for our future hope since the beginning of time (Titus 1:2). When we know, love, and follow the Lord, we can put all our spiritual estate planning in his loving hands and rest assured that we'll be taken care of and embraced when that future becomes today!

Lesson 4

Kids are beings of the here and now. The closest they come to planning for the future is what to do next Saturday. But kids are often frightened of the unknown, and when their feelings become distraught or filled with doubt, they need to remember that God has things under control and freely gives us a future and a hope. Use this lesson to help kids realize that we do have hope today and that our hope can never be taken away in the future.

POWER Focus

Before class cut an 8-by-10-inch piece of poster board. Then cut a 1-inch square from the center of the poster board. Tape the poster board rectangle to the top of a colorful magazine picture and trim any excess magazine from the edges. The poster board rectangle should flop over the magazine picture, revealing only the picture in the small peeking square. During the activity, you'll flip the poster board back to reveal the entire picture.

Welcome kids and let them know how glad you are that they're in class. Gather kids in a circle and hold up the poster-board rectangle with the peeking square in place. Ask kids to tell what they think they see or what this is a picture of.

After several responses, say: **It's tough to tell what the whole picture contains when we have only a small peek at it. Looking at our future can seem this way too. We have only glimpses into what the future may hold because we can't see the whole picture. There are days and times when we have troubles, frustrations, and feel hopeless. It seems impossible to look toward the future when we only see the small piece called "today." But God sees the whole picture! And God calls us to have hope because he is already in the future and joyously knows what is there for us.** Ask:

★ How does seeing only today limit us from knowing the future?

★ How do faith, trust, and hope that things will get better in the future help us get through tough times today?

Flip back the poster board to reveal the entire picture. Say: **See? When we know what the whole picture holds, we can understand the small pieces and what they mean! Isn't it wonderful that God sees the whole picture—both today and in the future? Today we'll discover how relying on God and having hope can get us through tough times and lead us to a promising, happy future. We'll learn that God has**

Lesson 4

promised us a hope and a future that can never fade away. And we'll begin learning a new Mighty Memory Verse about the power of hope. Right now, let's explore what God's Word tells us about our future and our hope.

THE MIGHTY MESSAGE

Before class, find a 3-pound chunk of dry ice from a vending supply company (if necessary, look in the yellow pages for a supplier in your area). Dry ice is relatively inexpensive and will make this activity extremely memorable for kids! Simply wrap the dry ice in thick layers of newspaper and keep it in a cooler until the beginning of class or this activity. (Dry ice will evaporate in a couple of hours, depending on the size of the chunk.) Then, using gloves, unwrap the dry ice and plop it in an empty cooking pot and set the pot on the floor at one end of the room. Let the dry-ice mist curl and snake over the floor. This is the hazy, mysterious "future"! (Do not let children touch the dry ice at any time. When you're done with this activity, simply set the pot out of reach on a tall bookshelf.) If you choose not to use this awesome special effect, simply scatter fiberfill at one end of the room on the floor for a "hazy future."

You'll also need to unroll a length of shelf paper from one end of the room to the area you're calling the "future." Tape the paper in place. One more preparation (hang in there, this is an awesome activity and well worth it!): copy the six Future Cards from page 124 and cut them out. Tape 2-foot lengths of white ribbon to the cards and place the cards inside the pot with the dry ice so the ribbons trail away from the pot. Kids will be pulling the ribbons to retrieve the cards from the "future." (Whew! Now you're ready for an awesome and memorable activity!)

Have kids stand at the end of the room opposite the dry ice, then ask a child to write the word "past" on the shelf paper. Say: **We'll pretend that we're standing in the past to remind us how God has been planning for our hope and future since the beginning of time.** Ask a volunteer to read aloud Titus 1:2, then say: **We've spent a few weeks learning about how**

POWER POINTERS

Kids are often afraid of the future or the unknown. Reassure them that God is already in the future and has promised we will have a future hope with him!

Lesson 4

God has laid a foundation for our hope since the beginning of time. How has God planned for our hope? Help kids review and list on the shelf paper that God has given us hope through his promises, through sending Jesus, and through the Holy Spirit. Say: **God has given us a strong, powerful foundation of hope from the past. Now let's hop forward to the present!**

Lead kids in hopping forward to the center of the shelf paper. Invite a child to write "present" on the paper, then read aloud Psalms 33:11 and 131:3. Say: **The word *present* means today, right now. How is God giving us hope for our future, right now, today?** Lead kids to tell (and list on the shelf paper) that God is keeping his promises, teaching us his truth, giving the Holy Spirit to lead us, and loving and forgiving us through Jesus.

Then continue: **We have hope today because God is with us and because he planned for our hope in the past—and God's plans never disappoint us! Turn around and look at the past. We can learn today by seeing what happened in the past. We know God has kept his promises. We know he sent Jesus to love and forgive us. We can look and learn from the past to have hope for today. Now, let's turn and face the future!**

Face toward the dry-ice "future" and quietly say: **The future is before us, and we haven't been there yet. It looks sort of hazy, doesn't it? But God is already in the future and is preparing a place for us. We can get close to the future and take a peek by reading what the Bible tells us about tomorrow. Tiptoe closer to the dry ice, but stop short of it.** Have a child pull a ribbon to remove a card from the "future." Read the verse and briefly discuss how the verse fits into our future with God. Then write the phrases "God's purposes and plans," "good works," "eternal life," "heavenly home," and "blessings" at the end of the shelf paper closest to the future.

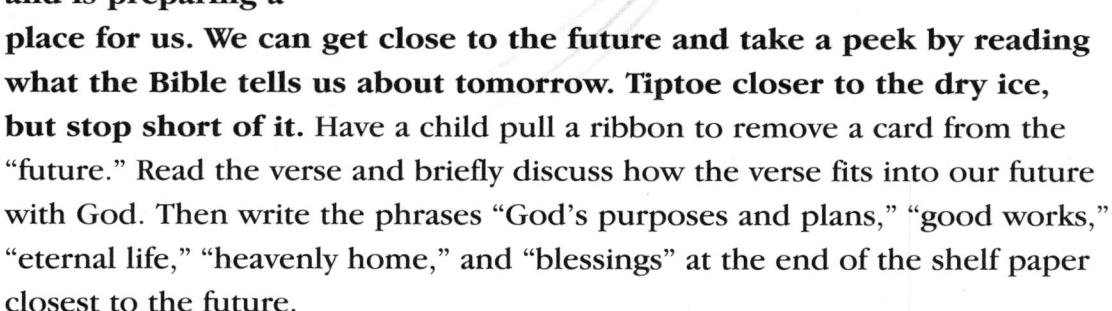

When all the cards have been read, say: **You see, we can have hope today because God has given us hope from the past and because God is**

41

Lesson 4

planning for our future! That gives me such joyous hope for today—in fact, our futures are so bright with the Lord, we need to wear sunglasses! Let's make some cool shades to wear as a reminder of the bright future and hope God gives us.

THE MESSAGE IN MOTION

Before class, photocopy on stiff paper the Cool Shades sunglasses pattern from page 124. (You'll need to enlarge the pattern to best fit the ages of the children in your class.) Make one copy for each child. (To shorten craft time if needed, cut out the sunglasses and lens openings before class.) You also need to cut small squares of red cellophane to fit the lens of the glasses. Kids will be taping or gluing the cellophane over the lens openings. Write the words to the rap from this activity on a piece of shelf paper and tape it to the wall for kids to read.

Hand each child a sunglasses pattern and cut out the glasses and lenses. Have kids use markers to write "My future's so bright with God" on one bow and "I gotta wear shades!" on the other. Explain that there was a popular song with a similar title, but we know our future and hope are so bright because we love and trust God. Tape red cellophane squares to the lens openings of the glasses on the side that faces the eyes. Then decorate the glasses using markers to make swirls, stars, hearts, or other shapes.

When the shades are done, have kids wear them as they clap and rap the words from the paper on the wall.

God has given me hope with the plans he's laid—
My future's so bright, I gotta wear shades!
God has given me a place in the future he's made—
My future's so bright, I gotta wear shades!
God has promised that our hope can't fade—
My future's so bright, I gotta wear shades!

Say: **Wow! We do have exciting futures filled with hope. God has**

promised us a hope and a future, and God always keeps his promises—just as his Word says! Let's learn more of God's Word with a new Mighty Memory Verse. Your cool new shades can help!

SUPER SCRIPTURE

Before class, use crayons to color a red 12-by-4-inch rectangle on white paper. (Make the red a medium hue, not scarlet or too light.) Now, using a blue crayon, lightly write the words to Proverbs 23:18 over the red in the rectangle so it's not obviously visible a foot away. (Remember the old Password game? This activity works on the same principle, with the red masking the blue until revealed by red cellophane paper—which is on the kids' glasses!) Flip the paper over and write the verse in blue crayon without using the red. Then tape the paper to the wall or a door, red side facing out.

Gather kids about a foot away from the paper and have them hold their shades. Say: **I have something special in this rectangle but it's hard to read, isn't it? The future can also be hard to "read" until God reveals it to us. Let's reveal what's written on this rectangle. Slip on your cool shades and see if you can read what has been written.** Have kids read Proverbs 23:18 using their glasses, then flip the paper over and read the verse three more times. Ask:

★ How do we know from this verse that we have a future hope?

★ Can our hope ever be taken away? Explain.

★ What hopes can we have for the future?

Say: **What a powerful verse giving us hope and assurance! We know two things from this verse. First, we do have a hope and a future, and second, our hope can never be taken away! We have hope right now and also for the future. Let's thank God for the future hope of eternal life, never-ending love, and a heavenly home he is preparing for us.** Keep the paper with the verse to use next week.

A POWERFUL PROMISE

Have kids sit in a circle. Say: **What an exciting time we've had! We've discovered that God is planning a future hope for us even today. We've learned that our hope can never be cut off or taken away and that it's very bright and joyous. And we began learning a new Mighty**

Lesson 4

Memory Verse that says (encourage kids to repeat Proverbs 23:18 with you), **There is surely a future hope for you, and your hope will not be cut off.**

Hold up the Bible and say: **God's Word teaches us that what God has promised, he will fulfill. Let's pass the Bible around our circle. When it's your turn to hold the Bible, you can say, "Thank you, God, for your promise of a future and a hope."** When everyone has had a turn, close with a prayer asking God to remind kids of their future and hope when things seem tough today. End with a corporate "amen."

If there's time, repeat the rap from the Message in Motion. Close with this responsive good-bye:

Leader: **May God's future hope be with you.**

Children: **And also with you!**

Distribute the Power Page! take-home papers as kids are leaving. Thank children for coming and encourage them to remember that they have hope that can never be taken away this week and forever. Let kids wear their Cool Shades home as reminders that our futures with God are so bright, we gotta wear shades!

Lesson 4   *Hope for Tomorrow*

POWER PAGE!

GOD'S GIFT

Solve the puzzle below, then read the circled letters to discover what gift God has freely given us.

Not near   ○ __ __

Opposite over   ○ __ __ __ __

A warty frog   ○ __ __ __

Rain protection   ○ __ __ __ __ __ __ __

Apple's color   ○ __ __

What hens lay   ○ __ __ __

Where we live   ○ __ __ __ __

Not closed   ○ __ __ __

Red & white   ○ __ __ __ __

Same as all   ○ __ __ __ __ __

FILL IT IN!

Look up Proverbs 23:18 and use the words to fill in the blanks.

(crossword grid with letters F, I, Y, F, H, N, O filled in)

The Whole Picture

We don't have the whole picture of our future, but God does! Finish the picture to show what you'd like the future to be like, then fill in the first part of Jeremiah 29:11.

"____ I _____ the _____ I _____ for you," _____ the _____. Jeremiah 29:11a

© 2001 by Susan L. Lingo.
Permission is granted to reproduce this page for ministry purposes only—not for resale.

Lesson 5

SAVING GRACE

Jesus gives us the hope of salvation and eternal life.

Romans 5:6, 8; 8:2
2 Thessalonians 2:16, 17
Titus 3:3-7

SESSION SUPPLIES

★ Bibles
★ gift wrap & tape
★ markers & scissors
★ small gifts (candies, pencils, erasers, etc.)
★ 2 black & 2 green balloons
★ a straight pin
★ construction paper
★ brown grocery sacks
★ white crayons
★ chenille wires
★ masking tape or red electrical tape
★ photocopies of Proverbs 23:18 (page 127)
★ photocopies of the Power Page! (page 53)

MIGHTY MEMORY VERSE

There is surely a future hope for you, and your hope will not be cut off. Proverbs 23:18

(For older kids, add in Jeremiah 29:11: "For I know the plans I have for you," declares the LORD, "plans to prosper you and not to harm you, plans to give you hope and a future.")

SESSION OBJECTIVES

During this session, children will
★ learn that Jesus' forgiveness and salvation are gifts of love
★ discover that the hope of salvation is for all people
★ explore how we can go from hopeless to hopeful
★ thank Jesus for the hope of salvation and eternal life

BIBLE BACKGROUND

Few things in our earthly world last, even though we may hope with all our hearts that they will. Cars fail, relationships flounder, even the hope of eternal spring gives way to summer's heat and autumn's fading colors. Isn't it wonderful that the hope we have through Jesus' gift of love and salvation is a living hope that can never fade away or be stolen from us? In the midst of bitter disappointments and fading hopes, our hope in Christ and eternal life moves forward to heavenly assurance. What a divine reminder of brighter days to come!

Lesson 5

Kids constantly hope for things—new bikes, better grades, extra spending money, closer friends. But as easily as they hope, they can become disappointed, bitter, and even cynical. Kids need to realize that hopes placed in Jesus are hopes fulfilled and will never disappoint us or disappear. Use this lesson to help kids understand that the gift of salvation given us through Jesus creates hope eternal and gives them a real reason to smile!

POWER FOCUS

Before class, wrap up a small gift for each child. Choose small wrapped candies, erasers, pencils, note pads, or magnets and wrap them in colorful gift wrap or tissue paper.

Welcome kids to class and tell them that you are glad they are present. Hold up a gift and say: **This will be such an exciting lesson that I'd like to begin by giving someone in our class a special gift.** Pause and look around the room, then continue: **This is a special gift, one I'm sure you'll enjoy, but who should I give this gift to? Hmm, it's so hard to decide! Why don't you close your eyes and place your hands in your laps, then don't peek until I tell you it's okay.**

While kids hide their eyes, quickly deliver a gift to each lap, then say: **Okay, you can look up and see who has the gift!** Have kids wait before opening their gifts. Say: **There was a gift for everyone here! What smiles I see—I can tell you're happy!** Ask:

★ How did it feel to know you might receive a special gift?

★ Did you hope you'd be chosen to receive the special gift? Explain.

Say: **Hope can be very exciting, especially when we know something special is involved. Did you know that Jesus has a gift for us too? This is a gift not just for one chosen person, but for anyone who accepts it! If it's exciting to hope for a gift in class, just think how much more exciting it is to know we have a gift from Jesus!**

Today we'll learn about the gift Jesus offers us and why we can have the hope and assurance of receiving it. We'll discover how we have gone from hopeless to hope filled, and we'll review our Mighty

Lesson 5

Memory Verse. Then later, you'll be able to open your gifts. First, let's explore what the Bible tells us about going from dark hopelessness to the joy of being hope filled!

THE MIGHTY MESSAGE

For this activity, you'll need two black balloons, two green balloons, and a straight pin. This is a great trick, but you may wish to try it before class! Slide a green balloon inside a black balloon, keeping the two openings together. Pull the green neck out a bit and inflate the green balloon inside the black one. Tie the end, but keep hold of it. Now blow the black balloon up so it's a bit larger than the green one. Tie the end along with the end of the green balloon into one knot. Trim any excess green away so it appears you have only a black balloon. During the activity, you'll prick the top of the black balloon (shallowly so you don't also pop the green balloon!) so it pops and reveals the green balloon. Quickly hide the black balloon. It will appear as if the black balloons has changed to green! Prepare one set of color-change balloons.

Gather kids in a group and set the black balloons to one side. Slide the straight pin into your sleeve to keep it handy. Say: **Let's see how we've gone from hopeless to hopeful by reading some important verses in the Bible. Listen for what made the difference and gave us hope as you follow along with my actions.** Paraphrase Titus 3:3-7 as follows:

At one time we were foolish and disobedient (shake your head). **We were filled with hate and treated each other in mean ways** (make silly faces at others). **We didn't deserve to be loved, and we were hopeless** (hang your head and shake it slowly). **But God loved us anyway and sent Jesus to love us too** (look surprised and happy). **Jesus came to love and forgive us and to die for our sins so we could be forgiven by God** (cover your heart with your hands). **It was through Jesus' love and forgiveness that we were reborn with hope and renewal by the Holy Spirit** (smile and hold arms upward toward heaven). **Through the gift of Jesus' love, forgiveness, salvation, and**

POWER POINTERS

This is a good time to have a children's pastor or other church leader come in to chat with kids about accepting Jesus into their lives and reaffirming the hope they have in Christ.

grace we've received the gift of hope and eternal life! (Give others high fives.)

Say: **Wow! We went from hopeless and disobedient to having hope for eternity! That's pretty awesome, isn't it?** Ask:

★ **How did Jesus take us from hopeless to hope filled?**

★ **What gift does Jesus offer anyone who loves and accepts him?**

★ **How do Jesus' love, forgiveness, and salvation bring us hope?**

Say: **See how we've gone from being hopeless to having heavenly hope? We no longer need to feel sad and without hope.** Read aloud Romans 5:6, 8 and 8:2. Then hold up the color-change balloons. **Just as the Bible says, before Jesus comes into our lives we live in hopelessness. Things seem black and sad. But when we know, love, and follow Jesus** (pop the black balloon to reveal the green one), **we have a living hope that's as green and growing as a flower! We go from black hopelessness to the living hope of eternal life in Jesus. What a wonderful change! Let's see if you can go from feeling hopeless to hopeful in this next activity.**

THE MESSAGE IN MOTION

Before this activity, cut out a red construction-paper heart for each child and write the word "hope" on each heart. Cut a 3-by-4-inch black construction paper rectangle for each child. Use masking tape or red electrical tape to make a cross on a wall at one end of the room. Place the hearts below the cross, along with a tape dispenser.

Form three lines at the end of the room opposite the cross. Hand each child a black card and a white crayon. Challenge kids to write on the cards things that make them feel hopeless, discouraged, frustrated, or worried.

Lesson 5

Then have each team decide on a way they will travel to the cross, such as hopping, walking backward, tiptoeing, or walking heel-to-toe. Explain that in this relay, players will travel in the way their teams decided upon and take the black "hopeless" cards to the cross. Tape the cards to the cross and exchange them for hearts of hope. Then players will return to their lines carrying their hearts of hope so the next players can go. Continue until everyone has exchanged hopelessness for hearts of hope.

Read aloud Romans 8:2, then say: **Sin and death left us hopeless and feeling sad, but Jesus' gift of salvation has brought us hope. Whenever you have feelings of doubt or hopelessness, talk to Jesus and leave those feelings with him. We need to exchange those hopeless feelings for the living hope Jesus freely gives us! Now let's review the hope we have through God's Word as we review the Mighty Memory Verse. Hold on to your hearts of hope; we'll use them in a moment.**

SUPER SCRIPTURE

Before class, photocopy the Scripture strip for Proverbs 23:18 from page 127. You'll need one strip for each child. Collect a brown paper grocery sack for each child, several chenille wires, and green construction paper. Be sure you have the verse on newsprint from last week taped to the wall where kids can read it.

Gather kids by the verse on the wall and repeat Proverbs 23:18 three times aloud. Then cover up portions of the verse and see if kids can repeat the verse. Ask:

★ **In what ways did Jesus' salvation bring us a future hope?**

★ **Why can our hope never be cut off or be taken away?**

★ **How does knowing you have eternal hope get you through problems today?**

Say: **The hope that comes from Jesus is called a "living hope." That means our**

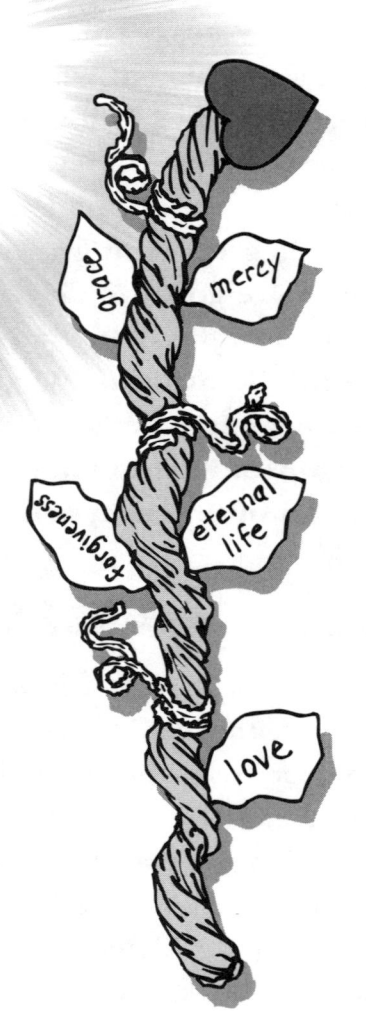

Lesson 5

hope is alive, growing, and helps us get through times that seem difficult. Let's make a living vine to remind us of the living hope we have in Jesus.

Show kids how to cut the bottoms from their paper sacks and twist the paper into gnarly "vines." Twist chenille-wire tendrils around the vines. Tear green-paper leaves and write the following words on some of the leaves: "love," "forgiveness," "eternal life," "mercy," and "grace." Tape Scripture strips to the backs of the red hearts of hope from the previous activity, then tape the hearts to the tips of the vines.

Say: **Hang your vines in your rooms to remind you of the living hope we have through the gift of Jesus' love and salvation. And repeat your Mighty Memory Verse each day to remind you that your hope can never be taken away! Now we can offer a prayer of thanks for the gift of hope we have in Jesus, then you can open your other special gifts.**

A POWERFUL PROMISE

Gather kids and say: **Today we've learned that Jesus' gift of salvation has taken us from hopeless to hopeful assurance of eternal life. We've discovered that Jesus' gifts of salvation and hope are for everyone. And we reviewed the Mighty Memory Verse, which says, "There is surely a future hope for you, and your hope will not be cut off." Proverbs 23:18.** (Repeat Jeremiah 29:11 with older kids.)

Hold up the Bible and say: **God's Word teaches us that we have hope through Jesus' gift of salvation, love, and forgiveness. Let's pass the Bible around the circle. When it's your turn to hold the Bible, you can say, "Jesus, my hope is in you!"** Continue until everyone has had a turn to hold the Bible. Then end with a prayer thanking Jesus for being our living hope and for bringing us the hopeful assurance of eternal life. Let kids open their small gifts.

Lesson 5

Read aloud 2 Thessalonians 2:16, 17. Then end with this responsive good-bye:

Leader: **May Jesus' hope and love be with you.**

Children: **And also with you!**

Distribute the Power Page! take-home papers as kids are leaving. Thank children for coming and encourage them to remember the hope they have in Jesus during the week. Remind kids to take home their gifts and vines.

Lesson 5   **Hope for Tomorrow**

POWER PAGE!

FRIENDLY Q & A

Fill in the words to Ephesians 2:8 to see how you have been saved. Then solve the puzzle at the bottom to discover what God's great grace is.

For it is by __ __ __ __ __ you have
              5   3

__ __ __ __ __ __ __ __, through
  2   9

__ __ __ __ __ —and this __ __ __ from
8 4   10

__ __ __ __ __ __ __ __, it is the
      1 11   6

gift of __ __ __.
          7

Grace is

__ __ __ __ __ __ __ __ __ __ __
1 2 3 4 5 2 6 7 8 4 9 10 11

Try This!

Make this cool tool to teach your family and friends about going from hopeless doubt to a hopeful heart.

1. Take a matchbox and tape a small piece of cardboard to the center box bottom.
2. Write "hopeless" on a small piece of paper and place it in one half of the box bottom.
3. Make a ♥ to fit in one half of the box bottom. Write "hope" on the ♥.
4. Show your audience how we might feel hopeless at times. Slide the hopeless paper into the box and close it.
5. Be sneaky and turn the box so no one sees. When you slide it open, pull out the ♥ of hope Jesus gives us through his love and salvation.

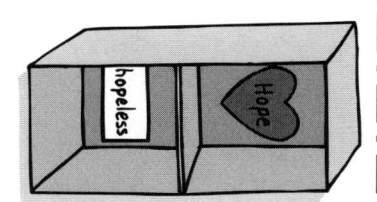

LETTER BEFORE

Write the letter that comes <u>before</u> the letter under each space to complete the Mighty Memory Verse.

__ __ __ __ __   __ __   __ __ __ __ __ __   __   __ __ __ __ __ __   __ __ __ __
U I F S F   J T   T V S F M Z   B   G V U V S F   I P Q F

__ __ __   __ __ __,   __ __ __   __ __ __ __   __ __ __ __   __ __ __ __
G P S   Z P V   B O E   Z P V S   I P Q F   X J M M

__ __ __   __ __   __ __ __   __ __ __   __ __ __ __ __ __ __ __   23:18
O P U   C F   D V U   P G G   Q S P W F S C T

© 2001 by Susan L. Lingo.
Permission is granted to reproduce this page for ministry purposes only—not for resale.

Lesson 6

HOME OF HOPE

Even now Jesus is preparing a home for us with God.

John 14:1-3
1 Peter 1:3, 4
2 Peter 3:13
Revelation 21:11-21

SESSION SUPPLIES

★ Bibles
★ old building plans or blueprints
★ white shelf paper
★ markers & scissors
★ glitter glue & sequins
★ tape & glue
★ graham crackers
★ tube or canned icing
★ string licorice, raisins, gumdrops, etc.
★ paper plates & plastic knives
★ construction paper
★ photocopies of the Whiz Quiz (page 62) and the Power Page! (page 61)

MIGHTY MEMORY VERSE

There is surely a future hope for you, and your hope will not be cut off. Proverbs 23:18
(For older kids, add in Jeremiah 29:11: "For I know the plans I have for you," declares the LORD, "plans to prosper you and not to harm you, plans to give you hope and a future.")

SESSION OBJECTIVES

During this session, children will
★ learn that Jesus is preparing a new home for us
★ discover that our new home is a hope and assurance
★ explore what our new home, heaven, and earth will be like
★ express thanks for our future hope and home

BIBLE BACKGROUND

When most of us think about our futures, we project months or years ahead. We think of our futures in terms of retirements, pensions, and where we'll choose to live when tomorrow arrives. As Christians, we can project even further into the future and enjoy the joyous hope that comes from contemplating a different kind of retirement home—our heavenly home. Even now, it gives us great comfort and hope to know that Jesus is preparing a place for each of us with our loving Father in his heavenly mansion.

Lesson 6

Ask kids if they want to move to a new home in a new city, and most will balk at the prospect. Even in this amazingly mobile society, most kids don't relish moves—and it's no wonder. There's love and great security in that familiar house down the block they call "home." But it's important for kids to realize that Jesus is preparing a heavenly home for them even now: a home filled with God's love and perfect security that can never be taken away. Use this lesson to help kids understand that the home of hope Jesus is preparing for us is the perfect home to spend eternity surrounded by love, life, and never having to move again!

POWER focus

Before class, find a set of old building plans or blueprints to show kids. Check with local architects or building contractors for old plans. Tape the plans to a wall or door for kids to see. Cut a 10-by-12-inch length of white shelf paper for every two or three kids.

Welcome kids to class with warm smiles and gather them in front of the building plans. Ask kids if they know what the drawing is used for, then ask:

★ **Why do you think builders need clear and detailed plans?**

★ **How do plans for building a house help accomplish the hopes of the builder? the people who will live in the house?**

Form pairs or trios and give each small group a sheet of white shelf paper and several markers. Challenge kids to draw a design for what they consider the "perfect" clubhouse or playhouse. You might spark the creative juices by mentioning that your idea of a perfect clubhouse would include a slide from the top level to the lower level and that there would be carousel horses to sit on instead of chairs. There might even be an indoor pond that holds giant goldfish! Encourage kids to work together to communicate their plans to one another and to be ready to explain why they added the features they chose. As kids work, make comments such as "Building for the future is fun and gives us hope!" and "Faith helps us accomplish what hope imagines!"

After five minutes, have kids come back to the large group and allow each small group a few moments to show and explain their building plans. Then ask:

★ **In what ways are building plans like promises for the future?**

★ **Why must future hope be carefully planned for?**

Lesson 6

Say: Anyone building a new home needs to make careful preparations. If not, the builder won't meet the hopes and plans of the people who will enjoy living there. Did you know that even now Jesus is preparing a new home for us in heaven? Today we'll learn about the new home and new heaven the Lord is preparing for us and in which we can put our hopes. We'll discover that our future home in heaven is a hope that can never fade away, and we'll review our Mighty Memory Verse. But first, let's do a little building preparation ourselves as we discover what God's Word tells us about our future home.

THE MIGHTY MESSAGE

Before this activity, cut a 3-foot length of white shelf paper and tape it to the floor. Set craft materials around the paper, including glue, tape, glitter glue, sequins, and markers. Kids will be making an embellished poster of a new heaven and earth on the paper to display on a bulletin board or hall for everyone to enjoy. Select a place to display your poster before class so kids can have the enjoyment of hanging their display themselves!

Form three groups and position kids so one group is at the left side of the paper, one is below the paper, and one is at the right side. Say: **The Bible tells us a lot about what our new home in heaven will be like and what the new earth will be like as well.** The group on the left of the paper will be drawing our new home in heaven. The group on the right will be making the new city. And the group below the paper will be drawing happy, hopeful faces to show how great our hope in a new heaven and earth

POWER POINTERS

Use hot glue to attach satin cords to the cute houses from Monopoly. Embellish them with glitter to make neat necklaces that remind kids of their hope for a heavenly home!

is. Let's see what the Bible teaches about what our future home will be like.

Invite members from group one (new home) to read aloud John 14:1-3. Point out that Jesus tells us that the home he is preparing for us even now has many rooms and that we'll live with him forever in that beautiful mansion! Then have kids in group one quickly draw the outline of a large house with many rooms (a cross-section drawing will be easiest).

Have kids in group two (new city) read aloud Revelation 21:11, 18, and 21. Point out that the new city on earth will be glorious and made of precious jewels and gems. Have kids quickly draw a rough outline of a city with a street going through it on the opposite side of the paper from the house. Suggest that kids draw "glow lines" around the city to show how brightly the gems and gold will shine.

Have kids from group three (new hope) read aloud 1 Peter 1:3, 4 and 2 Peter 3:13. As kids quickly draw several smiling faces across the bottom of the page, remind kids that our hope for a new home can never fade away because Jesus promised us this heavenly home.

Say: **God's Word tells us that our new home in heaven will have many rooms and that we can live there with the Lord. The new city on earth will be for God's glory and will shine like the sun! What bright hopes we have that can never perish or spoil. We can decorate our beautiful poster, then hang it in a place to remind others of the future hope we all have when we know, love, and follow Jesus.**

Lesson 6

Let kids use markers, glitter, and sequins to embellish their drawings. Have group one write: "A new home (John 14:1-3)" above the home they drew; group two write: "A new city (Revelation 21:11-21)" above the city they made; and group three write: "A new hope (2 Peter 3:13)" above the smiling faces they drew.

When the poster is complete, hang it in your chosen display spot.

Say: **What a powerful reminder of our hope for a new home! Now let's have a bit of fun building some delicious, edible homes to enjoy.**

THE MESSAGE IN MOTION

Before class, collect the ingredients to make cute, edible houses kids can take home. Set out paper plates, plastic knives, graham crackers, and the other edibles. Each child will need 2½ double graham-cracker rectangles (5 graham-cracker squares).

Explain to kids that they'll be preparing adorable, edible houses from graham crackers and other goodies. Have kids assemble their houses on paper plates and make four walls held together with icing "mortar." Add icing to the top four edges of the houses and set on graham-cracker roofs. Embellish the houses using bits of string licorice, raisins, and gumdrops (which can be snipped with clean scissors). As you work, discuss why our having hope for a future home with Jesus gives us hope today.

When the houses are complete, have a parade of homes and let kids view each other's home preparations. (Remind kids not to touch each other's houses.) Tell kids they can take their special homes home to share with their families just as Jesus will share his home with us. Say: **We can learn so much about hope and our future home by reading and learning God's Word. Let's review what God's Word says about our hope that can never be cut off.**

Lesson 6

SUPER SCRIPTURE

Be sure you have the verse on newsprint from last week taped to the wall for kids to read. Cut sheets of construction paper in half the long way and write the words from Proverbs 23:18 along with the reference on the paper strips, one word per strip. (You'll need 17 paper strips.) Trim excess paper from the ends of the words.

Repeat Proverbs 23:18 two times aloud. (If you are also learning Jeremiah 29:11, repeat this verse two times also.) Then have kids take turns covering up portions of the verse and challenging others to repeat the verse with the missing parts. Then ask:

★ How does a new home in heaven fit into our future hope?

★ How does it help our hope, faith, and trust to know that the hope of our heavenly home can never be taken away?

Say: **When we know that we have a future hope and home, we can feel such joy and hope today! Even when things might seem dark or confusing, we can grab hold of the hope Jesus gives us and know that hope will last forever. Let's embellish the words to our Mighty Memory Verse, then add them to our special display.**

Let each child use glitter and sequins to decorate the letters in a word. (If you have fewer than seventeen kids, have some kids embellish two words.) Assemble the verse above your display, then stand back to admire your handiwork. Have kids repeat the verse once more, then say: **Let's end our time together by thanking God for our new home and the hope he gives us.**

A POWERFUL PROMISE

Gather kids and say: **We've been learning today that Jesus is even now preparing a new home in heaven for us with many rooms. We've discovered that we'll live with Jesus one day in happiness and love. And we've learned that our future hope can never be cut off. Join hands, and let's thank God for giving us such a perfect hope not just for today, but for eternity.** Pray: **Dear Lord, we're so thankful and joyous that you love us enough to prepare a home for us in heaven, where we'll live with you someday. Thank you for giving us hope to last a lifetime and beyond! We love you too. Amen.**

If there's time, photocopy on stiff paper the picture on page 60, one for each child. Let kids cut out the pictures and decorate them with markers.

Lesson 6

Then flip the card over and write "Even now Jesus is preparing a home for us with God" or their own message about the hope we have with Jesus. Challenge kids to present (or send) their "hopecards" to a family member of a friend sometime during the coming week.

Before kids leave, allow five or ten minutes to complete the Whiz Quiz from page 62. If you run out of time, be sure to complete this page first thing next week. The Whiz Quiz is an invaluable tool that allows kids, teachers, and parents see what kids have learned in the previous three weeks. Read aloud Colossians 1:3-5, then end with this responsive good-bye:

Leader: **May God's hope be with you forever.**

Children: **And also with you!**

Distribute the Power Page! take-home papers as kids are leaving. Thank children for coming and remind them to take home their special houses to share with their families along with reminders about the hope we have in Jesus.

A new home (John 14:1-3)

A new city (Rev. 21:11-21)

A NEW HOPE (2 Peter 3:13)

Lesson 6   *Hope for Tomorrow*

POWER PAGE!

OUR SUPER CITY!

What amazing sights there will be in the new Jerusalem the Bible describes! Draw matching lines to show what the city will be like.

Rev. 21:12	pearl gates
Rev. 21:18	God's light
Rev. 21:19	no nighttime
Rev. 21:21	city of gold
Rev. 21:23	12 angels on 12 gates
Rev. 21:21	foundation of sapphire
Rev. 21:25	street of gold

New Home of Hope!

Jesus is making a new home for us in heaven. Share the joy of your hope by making a new home for your winged friends.

Birdhouse Pot

Take a 6-inch clay pot and decorate it using permanent markers or paints made for pottery.

Use tacky craft glue to attach dried grasses, straw, or fluffy fiberfill to the inside of the pot.

Thread a 2-foot length of strong cord through the bottom of the hole and out the top. Tie the cord securely.

Hang your new birdie home in a tree or on a fence post.

MISSING VOWELS

Use the letters a, e, i, o, and u to complete the words to the **MIGHTY MEMORY VERSE**.

Th_r_ _s s_r_ly _ f_t_r_ h_p_ f_r y__, _nd y__r h_p_ w_ll n_t b_ c_t _ff.

Pr_v_rbs 23:18

© 2001 by Susan L. Lingo.
Permission is granted to reproduce this page for ministry purposes only—not for resale.

Section 2 Hope for Tomorr[ow]

WHIZ QUIZ

Color in Yes or No to answer the questions.

✓ God did not promise us a future.   YES   NO

✓ Hope cannot fade away.   YES   NO

✓ Jesus' salvation gives us hope.   YES   NO

✓ Jesus' forgiveness is not for everyone.   YES   NO

✓ Jesus is preparing a new home for us.   YES   NO

✓ There will be a new heaven and earth.   YES   NO

Word Bank Wonder

Use the words from the word banks to complete the MIGHTY MEMORY VERSE.

WORD BANK
you
hope
Proverbs
surely
your
not

_____ is _____ a _____

_____ for ____ , and

____ ____ will ____

___ ___ ___ .

_____ 23:18

WORD BANK
future
There
off
hope
be
cut

62

© 2001 by Susan L. Lingo.
Permission is granted to reproduce this page for ministry purposes only—not for resale.

Section 3

HOPE FOR TODAY

We have this hope as an anchor for the soul, firm and secure.
Hebrews 6:19

Lesson 7

THE HOPE ROPE

God helps us hold on to hope in the toughest of times!

Psalms 18:6; 33:20
Lamentations 3:21-23
Hebrews 6:19

SESSION SUPPLIES

- ★ Bibles
- ★ helium balloons
- ★ flour
- ★ uninflated balloons
- ★ curling ribbon
- ★ paper or plastic funnels
- ★ scissors & markers
- ★ a stapler and tape
- ★ ¼-inch sisal rope
- ★ newsprint & construction paper
- ★ photocopies of the Hope Rope poem box (page 68)
- ★ photocopies of Hebrews 6:19 (page 127)
- ★ photocopies of the Power Page! (page 71)

MIGHTY MEMORY VERSE

We have this hope as an anchor for the soul, firm and secure. Hebrews 6:19

SESSION OBJECTIVES

During this session, children will
★ understand that God's love and mercy never fail us
★ learn how faith and patience help us hold on to hope
★ explore ways to hold on to hope in hard times
★ discover that God gives us fresh hope each day

BIBLE BACKGROUND

Think for a moment about times you've felt at the end of your rope, your patience has been used up, or your hope feels gone. Notice how we describe a lack faith, hope, and patience in terms of being used up, gone, or swept away? We talk about hope as if it were a fuel tank running full to empty. As Christians, we sometimes need a reality check from Lamentations 3:22, 23: "Because of the LORD's great love we are not consumed, for his compassions never fail. They are new every morning." God fills our spiritual fuel tanks new and full each morning and every moment—before they run dry. Next time you're feeling low on hope, remind yourself that God's mercies never fail and that he refills and refuels our hope today and every day!

Kids often strike a peculiar stance, with one foot in yesterday and the other in tomorrow. They enjoy looking

Lesson 7

back to see how they've grown and are filled with plans for the future. But when worries, doubts, and hopeless feelings sneak up in the present, kids often feel helpless to do something today. They need the reassurance that God is the God of the here and now and offers them help and hope for this present moment. Use this lesson to remind kids that God planned for our hope in the past, promises a future hope, but also offers us help and hope today.

POWER focus

Before class, collect a helium balloon and uninflated balloon for each child. You'll also need to cut a 3-foot length of curling ribbon for each child. You'll need funnels for this activity; they can be made from sheets of paper or, for a bit less mess, use plastic funnels. Tie the helium balloons to the backs of chairs. (Note: for this activity, you'll need to be in a room without vaulted ceilings, or helium balloons will be hard to retrieve!)

Welcome kids to class and hand each child a helium balloon. Ask kids what will happen if you count to three and let the balloons go. After several responses, lead kids in counting to three and letting go of the balloons. Say: **Wow! The balloons just floated away, out of control.** As kids retrieve the balloons and sit in a circle holding the ribbons, ask:

★ **How are floating balloons like we might feel when we're hopeless, out of control, and floating away from God?**

★ **How can hope and love anchor us and keep us from drifting too far from God?**

Say: **These balloons remind us what it can be like to feel hopeless and like we're floating out of control and maybe even away from God. When we feel hopeless, we need an anchor to keep us firmly in place. Listen to what the Bible tells us is an anchor for the soul.** Read aloud Hebrews 6:19, then say: **Hope is an anchor for the soul that is firm and secure. Hope keeps us close to God and anchored in his strength and helpful power. Let's make anchors for our balloons, then we'll discover how hope anchors us and secures us to God. We'll learn that God's love and mercy never fail us and are renewed every day to give us even more hope.**

Show kids how to work in pairs to roll paper cones (or use plastic funnels) and to pour flour into the uninflated balloons to make "anchors." Fill the balloons with flour until they're the size of golf balls, then knot the

Lesson 7

ends. Tie the ends of the ribbons around the colorful anchors, then let the balloons go. Point out how the anchors hold the balloons securely in one spot, just as hope anchors our souls to God. Set the balloons aside until later in the lesson.

THE MIGHTY MESSAGE

Before class, cut ¼-inch sisal rope into 2-foot lengths, one per child. Tie the ends of the ropes to a chair in the center of the room so they radiate outward. Place a Bible on the chair to represent God's truth.

Have kids hold the ends of the ropes as you say: **Have you ever felt hopeless, maybe as though you're at the end of your rope? Frustrations, problems, fights with friends and family members, and even tests in school or other worries can make us feel as if we're at the end of our ropes. What can we do when we feel hopeless? How can we hold on to that rope and find hope? Let's find out! I'll read some verses from the Bible. When you know how we can find hope, grab hold of the rope and pull yourself closer to the chair, which holds God's Word.**

Read aloud Psalm 18:6 and, when kids have moved forward, ask them to tell that calling on God for help gives us hope. Then say: **Calling on God through prayer brings us fresh hope in a powerful way. God hears our pleas for help and will answer us every time. Our prayers bring hope!**

Read aloud Psalm 33:20 and, when kids have moved forward again, ask them to tell that we find hope through waiting on God's power and help. Say: **Waiting on the Lord and having patience can bring us hope. God does all things in his time and in his way, and it's up to us to hold on and patiently wait on the Lord. Both prayers and patience bring us hope.**

Read aloud Jeremiah 31:17a and, when kids have reached the chair, have them tell that we find hope through God's promise for a future. Say: **We've learned that God has promised us hope and a future, and we know that God is faithful and keeps his promises. We find hope through prayer, patience, and God's promises!**

POWER POINTERS

Consider bringing in a real boat anchor for kids to try and lift. Explain that the weight keeps boats anchored in place, just as faith and hope anchor us in the Lord.

Have kids untie their ropes and sit in place. Ask:
* ★ What are things that make us feel hopeless?
* ★ In what ways can trusting God and asking for his help give us hope?
* ★ How does receiving God's hope and help show us we're loved by God?

Say: **Because God loves you, he wants you to have hope and not feel as though you're at the end of your rope. God provides ways for us to hold on to hope even in the toughest of times. When we pray for God's help, have patience in God's answer, and rely on God's faithful promises, we discover powerful hope that never fails us! Isn't that awesome? When we love God, we're never without hope.**

Read aloud Lamentations 3:21-23, then say: **See? God renews our supply of hope every day, so each morning when you get up and face a new, bright day, you can thank God for the hope he freely gives. God's hope anchors us in secure love just as a ship is anchored to the dock. Let's tie some ship's knots in our ropes as we discover more about the never-ending hope God gives us today!**

THE MESSAGE IN MOTION

Before this activity, photocopy the Hope Rope poem box on page 68, one copy per child. Kids will be tying simple overhand knots in their ropes. If you have older kids who might enjoy a challenge, invite a Boy Scout or "nautical" adult in to demonstrate how to tie four different kinds of knots, but be sure to cut extra-long lengths of rope, since fancier knots require more length.

Have kids sit facing you and holding their ropes. Slowly demonstrate how to tie a simple overhand knot, then have kids follow along, step by step. Tie four knots down the lengths of the ropes. Space the knots along the rope so they're several inches apart.

When the four knots are tied, have kids cut out four construction-paper circles, then use permanent markers to write the letters H, O, P, E on the circles, one letter per circle. Instruct kids to glue the circles on the

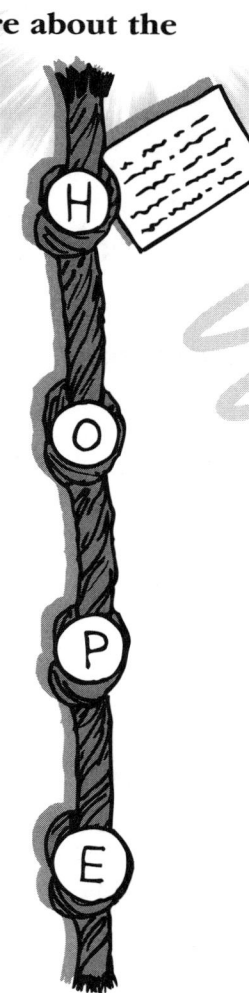

Lesson 7

knots. Then hand kids the Hope Rope boxes and staple or tape them to the tops of the ropes. Read aloud the poem and have kids point to each letter on their knots as it's read.

After the poem has been read, say: **Our Hope Ropes remind us that when we love and follow God, we're never at the end of our ropes or are truly hopeless. When you're feeling frustrated, sad, or full of worries, remember to ask for God's help, hold on to faith, have patience, and rely on God's everlasting promises! Then read the verses on your Hope Rope, and you'll find the hope you need in God! Scripture also helps us have powerful hope, so let's begin learning a new Mighty Memory Verse to remind us of the hope we find in God's Word.**

HOLD ON TO HOPE!

Ask for God's **H**elp through powerful prayer—

Hold **O**n to faith—not just thin air!

Trust and have **P**atience that God is right there—

Claim his **E**verlasting promises to which you are heir!

(Read Titus 3:7 and Lamentations 3:21-23)

SUPER SCRIPTURE

Before class, write Hebrews 6:19 on newsprint and tape it where kids can read the verse. Write the words to the Hope Song on newsprint and tape the words beside the verse. You'll also need copies of the Scripture strip for Hebrews 6:19 (page 127) for each child.

Gather kids in front of the verse and read Hebrews 6:19 aloud three times. Say: **Remember our floating balloons? What finally held them securely in place?** Let kids tell it was the weighted anchors that held the balloons, then continue: **We added anchors to our balloons to keep them rooted in place. God's truth keeps us rooted in hope by anchoring us in firm and secure ways.** Have kids hold their balloons and anchors, then toss the balloons in the air and watch as the anchors pull them down and hold them firmly to the ground.

Say: **When we feel out of control and hopeless, God's love, truth, powerful help, and mercy anchor us firmly in hope. Let's add the Mighty Memory Verse to our balloons as a reminder of being anchored in hope from the Lord.**

Staple the Scripture strips to the ribbons on the balloons. Say: **We've learned how God's love and help are like a ship's anchor holding us firmly in hope. And we tied ship's knots in our Hope Ropes to remind us how to find hope in tough times. Now let's sing a boat song to remind us of our Mighty Memory Verse.** Lead kids in singing The Hope Song to the tune of "Row, Row, Row Your Boat."

THE HOPE SONG

H-O-P-E hope!
An anchor for my soul—
Firm and secure, perfect and pure,
God's hope will keep me whole!

After singing the song three times, say: **Let's use our colorful balloons and anchors in offering a prayer thanking God for helping us find hope today.** Keep the Scripture verse on newsprint to use next week.

A POWERFUL PROMISE

Have kids stand in a circle and set their balloons in front of them. Say: **We've learned today that God wants us to have hope right now, in this moment, and that he will help us find the hope we need. We've discovered that**

Lesson 7

prayer, patience, and God's promises help us have hope in the hardest of times. And we began learning a new Mighty Memory Verse that says (encourage kids to repeat Hebrews 6:19), **"We have this hope as an anchor for the soul, firm and secure."** Now let's use our balloons to offer a prayer of thanks to God for giving us hope that never fails us. Follow along with your balloons as I pray.

Dear Lord, we embrace the hope you freely give us (gently hug the balloons). **We're so thankful that you hold us with love** (hold the balloons close to the floor) **and that, as our prayers rise to you** (release the balloons so they float upward), **you answer us and keep us firmly held in hope as an anchor holds a ship. We love you, God** (hug the balloons), **and thank you for the hope we have each day. Amen.**

Read aloud Psalm 146:5, 6. Then end with this responsive good-bye:

Leader: **May God's hope be with you today and always.**

Children: **And also with you!**

Distribute the Power Page! take-home papers as kids are leaving. Thank children for coming and encourage them to use their Hope Ropes whenever they feel hopeless and sad.

Lesson 7 **Hope for Today**

POWER PAGE!

Hope-n-Help

Read the verse on the left and match it to the way God helps and gives us hope on the right.

Psalm 18:6 — God is our shield.

Psalm 33:20 — God promised us a future.

Psalm 146:5, 6 — God hears our prayers.

Jeremiah 31:17 — God loves us all.

Lamentations 3:22 — God is faithful.

HOME HOPE ROPE

This neat door hanger lets everyone know your hope is in the Lord!

Whatcha need:
- a length of thick sisal rope (½-inch by 3-foot)
- 3 jingle bells
- twist-tie wires
- fabric paints

Whatcha do:
1. Tie 4 overhand knots in the rope. (Leave 3 inches of rope after the last knot.)
2. Fray the bottom pieces of rope and tie 3 jingle bells to the frayed rope.
3. Paint the knots and paint the words "Hope in God" between the knots.
4. Add a twist-tie wire to the top knot and hang your special rope on the front door!

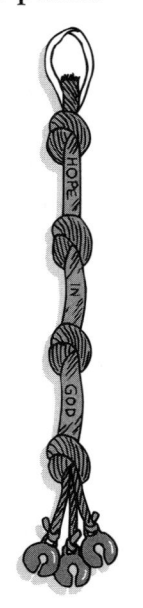

Crazy Circuit Board

Follow the arrows to plug in the missing letters from Hebrews 6:19.

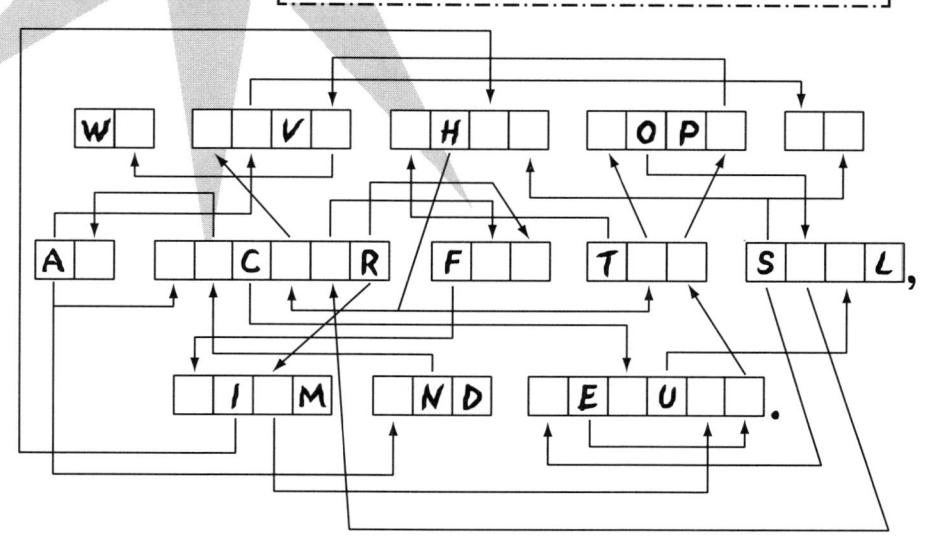

W _ _ V _ H _ _ O P _ _

A _ C _ R _ F _ T _ S _ L,

_ I _ M _ N D _ E _ U _ .

© 2001 by Susan L. Lingo.
Permission is granted to reproduce this page for ministry purposes only—not for resale.

71

Lesson 8

HEARTS OF HOPE

Serving God and others spreads hope and happiness.

Psalms 25:5; 33:20, 21
Romans 12:10-13
2 Thessalonians 2:16, 17

SESSION SUPPLIES

★ Bibles
★ construction paper
★ scissors & markers
★ newsprint
★ baby-food jars and lids
★ ribbon
★ small candies
★ tacky craft glue
★ paper punch
★ photocopies of the poem in the heart box (page 76)
★ photocopies of the Power Page! (page 79)

MIGHTY MEMORY VERSE

We have this hope as an anchor for the soul, firm and secure. Hebrews 6:19.
(For older kids who need a challenge, also work on learning Lamentations 3:22, 23a: "Because of the LORD's great love we are not consumed, for his compassions never fail. They are new every morning.")

SESSION OBJECTIVES

During this session, children will
★ realize that helping others gives us hope
★ understand that hopeful hearts are joyous
★ serve others by reminding them of God's love
★ discover that following God's Word gives us hope

BIBLE BACKGROUND

What's the quickest way to banish the blahs, ditch your doubts, or give hopeless feelings the ol' heave-ho? One of the best ways is through stepping out of ourselves and our own feelings and helping others instead! Focusing inwardly on our own problems can make us feel more hopeless than ever. But turning that focus, nervous energy, and worry in a new, outward direction guarantees a lighter heart in short order. As always, God's great wisdom shines clear and strong in Romans 12:10-13, where his Word tells us to be devoted to one another, patient in affliction, passionate in serving, and joyful in hope. Serving God and

Lesson 8

others brings a renewed sense of hope and love that not only spreads to others but also gives our own hope a joyful power boost!

One of the first things the parents of a toddler learns is the fine art of distraction. If a child focuses on wanting a cookie in the store, it helps to move his attention elsewhere and the cookie is soon forgotten. And who hasn't seen newspaper stories about troubled teens who change their lives through turning to help others? Kids can be taught to focus their troubles and feelings of hopelessness in a new direction through serving God and others. Use this lesson to encourage kids to discover renewed hope through embracing others.

POWER Focus

Before class, practice folding and cutting out linked hearts according to the illustrations in the margin to create five paper hearts linked in a row. Tape two sheets of construction paper end to end, making sure to tape both sides of the seam from end to end. Fold the strip in half from left to right, then fold this piece into thirds. (Fold the left edge over to make one third, then fold the right edge back and under to make the other two thirds.) Draw the heart outline on the paper, then cut. When you unfold the paper, you'll have five linked hearts! (Be sure to trim off the remaining half-heart from each end.) Kids will be cutting out their own paper hearts along with you in this activity.

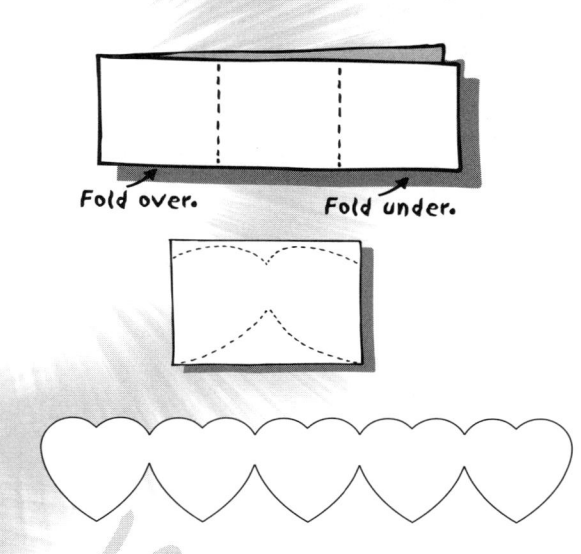

Welcome kids warmly to class and tell them that you're glad that they've come. Then ask kids to name things that spread or grow larger. Ideas might include weeds, clouds, puddles of spilled milk, and good news. Then say: **Lots of things begin small, then spread and grow larger. Good news, weeds, and spilled milk all begin small but soon spread all around. Two other things grow and spread too. Let's use paper and scissors to cut shapes as we discover what those things are.**

Hand kids sheets of construction paper, then show kids how to fold their papers and lightly trace the heart shapes on the folded papers. Then cut out

Lesson 8

the shapes and hold up the linked hearts. Say: **Wow! You cut out one heart, and look how it spread to make many hearts! Do you know why those hearts are linked? They're linked because of the hope they share. Love and hope are two things that can spread and grow to touch many people.**

Today we'll discover that spreading love by helping others also spreads hope—and makes us feel more hopeful ourselves. We'll learn that God wants us to help others and to spread his love and hope. And we'll review our Mighty Memory Verse that teaches us about hope as an anchor for the soul. Keep your paper hearts with you to use as we discover the recipe for hope and how we can spread that hope and make it grow.

THE MIGHTY MESSAGE

Before class, write Romans 12:10-13 on four sheets of newsprint, one verse per sheet.

Have kids form four groups and hand each group a verse. Explain that in this activity each group will read its verse and decide how they can use their paper hearts to act out what the verse says.

For example, Romans 12:10 could be acted out by having the kids use their hearts to "hug" the other kids as a sign of devotion or hold the hearts above the heads of other kids as a means of "honoring" them. Verse 11 might be acted out by waving the paper hearts as pom-poms in a lively cheer to represent zeal and fervor. (Explain these words to the group doing verse 11!) Verse 12 could be acted out by waving the hearts for joy, holding them still for patience, and kneeling with the hearts in "prayer." Finally, verse 13 might be illustrated by exchanging hearts with others or giving the hearts away.

After several minutes, have groups read their verses in order and act them out. Then read the verses once more in order without acting them out. Say: **What a great job you did acting out these very important verses! The recipe of hope includes being devoted to one another, serving God, being joyful and patient, and sharing with others.** Ask:

POWER POINTERS

For more awesome service projects that will make a difference in kids' lives, check out *101 Simple Service Projects Kids Can Do* from Standard Publishing!

Lesson 8

★ How can loving each other bring hope?
★ In what ways does serving God spread love and hope?
★ Why are joy, faith, and patience important ingredients in having hope?
★ How does sharing with others spread hope?

Have kids write the following words and symbols on their paper hearts, beginning with the hearts on the far left and going to the right: love, + serving, + joy, + sharing, = HOPE! When the hearts are done, read the recipe for spreading hope by reading the hearts from left to right. Then say: **When we begin with God's love and add serving, joy, and sharing, we discover a whole batch of wonderful hope to hold on to and also to share with others! Let's share a bit of hope right now by serving others as God desires.** Save the paper hearts to use later.

love + serving + joy + sharing = HOPE!

THE MESSAGE IN MOTION

Before class, collect small, clean baby-food jars with lids. You'll need one jar and lid for each child. You'll need small candies such as chocolate chips or cinnamon candies. Cut an 8-inch length of ribbon for each child. You'll also need a copy of the heart box (page 76) for each child. Decide in advance who you will present your service projects to, such as another kids' class or teen class at church. (Be sure to make enough jars for everyone in the other room!)

Let kids work in small groups and explain that you'll be making sweet reminders of God's hope as a way of helping kids in another class. Have kids glue a small pile of candies to the lids of the baby food jars, then set them aside to dry. Cut out the heart-shaped poem boxes and read the poem aloud. Punch holes at the tops of the hearts, then thread ribbon

75

Lesson 8

through the holes. Fill the baby-food jars with the small candies, then carefully screw on the lids. Tie the ribbons around the necks of the jars.

As kids work, remind them that God freely offers us hope today and that sharing the joy we have in our heavenly hope brings us even more hope! Point out that God wants us to serve others and to encourage them with hope. When the jars are done, set them aside to continue drying and read aloud Psalm 25:5.

Say: **Isn't it wonderful that so many things give us hope? Love, serving, sharing joy, God's promises, and even his Word bring us amazing hope today, right now! God's Word is truth, and it teaches us about having hope and sharing it with others. We can honor God by reviewing the Mighty Memory Verse we've been learning as we discover even more about the hope that anchors our souls and fills our hearts.**

When days seem dark
And it's hard to cope,
Remember that God
Is our sweet help and hope!

(Read Psalm 33:20, 21)

Lesson 8

SUPER SCRIPTURE

Be sure you still have the newsprint with Hebrews 6:19 written on it taped to the wall for kids to see.

Gather kids in front of the verse and repeat Hebrews 6:19 three times aloud. Then invite kids to cover up portions of the verse and challenge others to fill in the missing words as they repeat the verse. (If you have older kids, introduce the extra-challenge verse, then cover portions of this verse too). Continue until everyone has had a turn to hide a portion of the verse. Then ask:

★ **In what ways does hope anchor our hearts and souls in God?**

★ **How can we help others hold on to the powerful anchor of hope?**

Say: **This verse teaches us that hope isn't just a nice feeling to have—it does something powerful for us. Hope anchors our souls firmly and securely and keeps us close to God. Hope becomes an active part of our faith in God and how we trust him to help us in his time. Having hope gives us firm, secure faith in the Lord! Let's sing the Hope Song we learned last week. Sing with joy to the Lord as a thank-you for the hope he freely gives us today.**

Lead kids in singing the Hope Song to the tune of "Row, Row, Row Your Boat." Sing the song two times, then sing it as a round.

THE HOPE SONG

H-O-P-E hope!
An anchor for my soul—
Firm and secure, perfect and pure,
God's hope will keep me whole!

After singing, say: **Let's thank God for giving us a hope to share with others. Then we'll present our special projects to others who may need a reminder about the hope they have in God today and always.** Keep the Scripture verse on newsprint to use next week.

A POWERFUL PROMISE

Gather kids in a circle and have them hold their paper hearts from earlier in the lesson. Point to each heart as you say: **We've been learning today**

Lesson 8

that because God *loves* us, he gives us hope. We've discovered that *serving* others is a wonderful way to increase our own feelings of hope that bring us great *joy*. And we've seen how sharing love and helping others spreads *hope* just as God desires. As we go around the circle, you can thank God for one of the things written on your hearts. I'll go first to show you. Pray: **Dear God, I thank you for helping me serve you and others.** Continue around the circle until everyone has had a turn to thank God using her paper hearts.

Present your sweet projects to another class and have your kids read their recipes for hope from their paper hearts.

Read aloud 2 Thessalonians 2:16, 17. Then end with this responsive good-bye:

Leader: **May hope fill your hearts and overflow to others.**

Children: **And also you!**

Distribute the Power Page! take-home papers as kids are leaving. Thank children for coming and encourage them to look for ways to encourage others and share their hope this week.

Lesson 8   **Hope for Today**

POWER PAGE!

Hope from the Heart!

Read Romans 12:10-13 to discover how the good things in our hearts help us hold on to hope. Then use the key below to crack the message at the bottom.

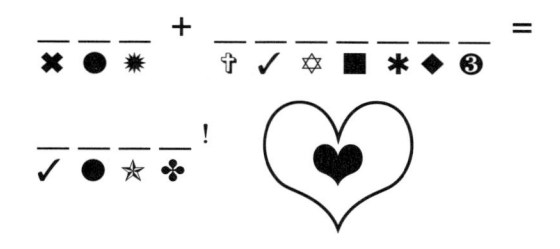

A	E	G	H	I	J	L
✡	♣	❸	✓	*	✖	◇

N	O	P	R	S	V	Y
◆	●	☆	■	†	♥	✺

___ ___ ___ ___ + ___ ___ ___ ___ ___ ___ ___ +
◇ ● ♥ ♣   † ♣ ■ ♥ * ◆ ❸

___ ___ ___ + ___ ___ ___ ___ ___ ___ ___ =
✖ ● ✺   † ✓ ✡ ■ * ◆ ❸

___ ___ ___ ___ !
✓ ● ☆ ♣

Hope Cakes

Serve someone in a sweet way with these cheery treats! Invite an adult to help and share in the fun.

You'll need:
★ ice-cream cones ★ cake mix
★ canned icing   ★ cupcake pan
★ candy hearts or ★ candy sprinkles
   jelly beans

Directions:
1. Prepare cake mix according to the package directions. Preheat the oven.
2. Pour batter into ice-cream cones, filling them ¾ full.
3. Poke a candy heart or jelly bean into the middle of the batter.
4. Carefully place cones in a cupcake pan. Bake according to package directions.
5. Cool and frost, then decorate.

SCRIPTURE SCRAMBLER

Unscramble the words in the word bank to complete Hebrews 6:19.

___ ___ ___ ___ ___ ___ ___ ___ ___ ___

___ ___ ___ ___ ___ ___ ___ ___ ___

___ ___ ___ ___ ___ ___ , ___ ___ ___ ___ ___ ___ ___

___ ___ ___ ___ ___ ___ ,

WORD BANK

eW
charno
mirf
eursce
pohe
na
veha

teh
dan
rfo
tish
luos
sa

© 2001 by Susan L. Lingo.
Permission is granted to reproduce this page for ministry purposes only—not for resale.

79

Lesson 9

A HELPING OF HOPE

Peace is a gift we share with others.

Romans 12:13
2 Corinthians 9:8
Ephesians 2:10
1 Timothy 3:13

SESSION SUPPLIES

★ Bibles
★ plastic sandwich bags
★ packing peanuts
★ a bag of candy circus peanuts
★ index cards
★ tape & colorful permanent markers
★ scissors & glitter glue
★ white terry-cloth washcloths
★ tissue paper & ribbon
★ envelopes
★ newsprint
★ copies of the Scripture strip for Hebrews 6:19 (page 127)
★ photocopies of the Whiz Quiz (page 88) and the Power Page! (page 87)

MIGHTY MEMORY VERSE

We have this hope as an anchor for the soul, firm and secure. Hebrews 6:19.

(For older kids who need a challenge, also work on learning Lamentations 3:22, 23a: "Because of the LORD's great love we are not consumed, for his compassions never fail. They are new every morning.")

SESSION OBJECTIVES

During this session, children will
★ review how Jesus offers us heavenly hope
★ realize that Jesus wants us to share hope with others
★ explore ways to share our hope in Christ
★ discover how sharing hope strengthens our own hope

BIBLE BACKGROUND

What are the best things you've shared with others? Was it a special recipe your best friend admired, the sweet news of a birth in the family, or perhaps outgrown clothing given to a homeless shelter? When you think of all the times, things, and words we share with others, the shared joy of giving others hope and happiness ranks the highest. Think of how the angels joyously shared the good news of Jesus' birth with the lowly shepherds and how hope and joy filled their hearts. And remember how Mary ran to share the amazingly wondrous news of Jesus' resurrection with his followers? Sharing joy, excitement, and hope with others increases our own sense of happiness and strengthens hope inside our own hearts.

Kids like sharing, especially when the shared news or item brings others smiles, laughter, and good feelings. Kids who share outgrown clothing and toys with less fortunate people often comment on how these simple acts help them recognize what they have and be thankful for it. Use this exciting lesson to teach kids that one of the best ways to have hope in our own hearts is to share hope with others.

POWER focus

Before class, place twelve foam packing peanuts and two candy circus peanuts in a plastic sandwich bag for each child. You may wish to have a few extra bags ready in case there are visitors in class.

Welcome kids warmly and let them know you're glad they have come to share time together. Tell kids that you'll begin your fun time with a lively game called Dare to Share. Hand each child a sandwich bag and explain that in this game, kids are to share one packing peanut at a time with other players. But each time they give out a packing peanut, the person accepting it must give them two in return! Explain that players must accept peanuts when they're offered and that all players must freely give out their packing peanuts to others. Tell kids if all the packing peanuts are given away, they can give one of their candy circus peanuts to someone else and eat the other one. Finally, tell kids they will have three minutes to share their peanuts.

At the end of three minutes, call time and have kids sit in place holding their sandwich bags. Say: **Wow! There was a lot of sharing and giving going on in his game! Were you able to share all of your packing peanuts? Why or why not?** Kids will not have shared all the peanuts in their bags and will figure out that it's

Lesson 9

impossible to give away all their peanuts at the same time that they're accepting more! Ask:

★ What happened when you shared with someone?

★ How is this like receiving more blessings when we share God's blessings with others?

★ Is it possible to run out of blessings when we keep receiving more? Explain.

Let kids nibble their candy circus peanuts. Say: **Each time you shared, you received more in return. That's just how it is when we share what the Lord gives us! When we share the Lord's love, blessings, forgiveness, and hope, we receive even more in return. Today we'll discover why it's important to share our hope with others and that Jesus wants us to share the hope he gives us. And we'll make cool Wash-n-Wear Washcloths to share Jesus' hope.**

First, let's explore what the Bible teaches us about sharing the joy and hope we have today.

POWER POINTERS

If kids are really crafty, consider making Hope Soap Balls to accompany your washcloths. Whip soap flakes and small amounts of water until the consistency of thick dough. Form balls and dry on waxed paper.

THE MIGHTY MESSAGE

Before class, write the following words on index cards, one word per card: Who, What, When, Why, How.

Have kids form a large circle in the center of the room, then number off by twos (if your group is very large, number off by threes). Place one of the index cards face down in the center of the circle and be sure kids are standing at least five feet from the card.

Say: **In this lively game, I'll call out a one or a two and players with those numbers must walk heel-to-toe to try and be the first to snatch the card and read the word on it. Then I'll ask a question using that word and read a verse that gives a clue to the answer. The group who snatched the card has one try to answer the question. If you're right, you'll score a point for your team. If the answer is incorrect, the other team can try to answer and score. We'll continue until all the cards have been answered.**

Use the following questions and verses for the cards.

★ *Who* can we share our hope with? (Romans 12:13)

★ *What* does sharing our hope do for others and for us?
(1 Timothy 3:13)
★ *When* does the Lord help us share hope with others?
(2 Corinthians 9:8)
★ *Why* are we created new in Christ? (Ephesians 2:10)
★ *How* can we share the hope Jesus gives us? (Hebrews 10:24)

Add up the points and have the winning team give the other players high fives. Then say: **Several weeks ago we learned that Jesus gives us hope through his forgiveness and sacrifice on the cross. Jesus gives us hope through salvation, love, forgiveness, and the hope of eternal life. And these are happy, helpful, powerful hopes he wants us to share with others. Just imagine if everyone felt the joy and hope we feel in Jesus! When we share the Lord's hope with others, God multiplies our hope even more, just as the peanuts in our game multiplied.**

Now, if God gives us more hope when we share with others, can we ever truly run out of hope and be hopeless? Never! God has promised us hope, and he always keeps his promises! Now let's share hope with others as we make Wash-n-Wear Washcloths and discover even more about our powerful, renewable resource from Jesus called hope!

THE MESSAGE IN MOTION

Before class, purchase a package or two of inexpensive white terry-cloth washcloths. Check discount stores for low, low prices on washcloths purchased in bulk. If possible, let kids make two cloths—one to share and one to keep. You'll also need colorful permanent markers and glitter glue. Write the poem on the following page on newsprint and tape it to a wall for kids to copy. Decide prior to class who will receive your special projects, such as another kids' class, an adult group, or the church staff. Be sure to make enough washcloths to share.

Invite kids to work in pairs or trios and hand each person a white washcloth to decorate, using bright-colored permanent markers and dabs of glitter glue. (Glue will need to dry quickly, so use it sparingly.) Suggest designs such

Lesson 9

as bright morning sunshine, stars, hearts, geometric patterns, and interesting squiggles. Have kids use permanent markers to write the following rhyming couplet on the backs of the cloths:

Jesus took our sins away
And gives us hope and help each day!
(1 Peter 1:3, 4)

As kids work, visit about ways to share hope, such as through prayer, telling others about Jesus, helping people, and speaking kind and encouraging words. Remind kids that God's Word tells us that his blessings, help, and hope are new each morning. Read aloud Lament-ations 3:22, 23.

When the projects are finished and the glue is dry, wrap them in tissue paper and add ribbon bows. Present your gifts to the class or adults who are to receive them and consider having kids sing the Hope Song.

THE HOPE SONG

H-O-P-E hope!
An anchor for my soul—
Firm and secure, perfect and pure,
God's hope will keep me whole!

Say: **God's Word tells us to share with others.** Now let's discover what else God's Word tells us about hope as we review the Mighty Memory Verse.

SUPER SCRIPTURE

Before this activity, be sure you still have the newsprint with Hebrews 6:19 written on it from the previous lessons. Copy the Scripture strip of the verse for every child, then cut each verse into ten pieces (without cutting words in two) and place the pieces in an envelope. Prepare a puzzle for each child. (If you have older kids who have been learning the extra-challenge verse, make a second set of puzzle pieces for each child using Lamentations 3:22, 23.)

Lesson 9

Have kids repeat Hebrews 6:19 three times aloud in unison, then distribute the puzzle envelopes. Explain that in this Scripture relay, kids must reassemble their verses but must share three puzzle pieces with three other players. If they need a particular piece, they can ask others for that piece. Remind kids that sharing and acceptance both take patience and kindness.

When the verses have been reassembled, have each child repeat the verse. Then ask:

★ **Why is it important to share Jesus' hope with others?**

★ **In what ways does sharing our hope draw us closer to Jesus? to others?**

★ **How can you share your hope with someone today? in the upcoming week?**

Say: **The Lord has given us such wonderful hope, and because our hope is renewed each morning we have hope enough to spread to others! We can offer a prayer of thanks for the hope we have and can share today.**

A POWERFUL PROMISE

Gather kids in a circle and say: **We've had an exciting time learning about the importance of sharing our hope with others and how God multiplies our hope when we share. We've discovered different ways to share the hope that Jesus gives us and have reviewed God's Word, which teaches us about hope being an anchor for our souls.** Repeat the Mighty Memory Verse (and the extra-challenge verse if you've been learning it).

Hold up the Bible, then say: **God's Word teaches us everything we need to know about hope and about sharing our hope with others so they might be anchored in the Lord as well. Let's pass the Bible around our circle. When you hold**

Lesson 9

the Bible, you can say, "I want to share my hope with others, Lord."
Continue passing the Bible until everyone has had a turn to hold it, then end with a corporate "amen."

Before kids leave, allow five or ten minutes to complete the Whiz Quiz from page 88. If you run out of time, be sure to complete this page first thing next week. The Whiz Quiz is an invaluable tool that allows kids, teachers, and parents see what kids have learned in the previous three weeks.

Read aloud 2 Thessalonians 2:14, then end with this responsive good-bye:

Leader: **May you always share your hope with others.**

Children: **And also you!**

Distribute the Power Page! take-home papers as kids are leaving. Thank children for coming and encourage them to look for ways to share their hope with someone this week.

Lesson 9   *Hope for Today*

POWER PAGE!

Scripture Share

Invite a family member or friend to share in the fun of learning what God tells us about sharing with others. Fill in the missing words, then draw lines to match the verse with the reference.

Rom. 12:13 — For we are God's _____ created in Christ Jesus to do _____ _____.

2 Cor. 1:7b — Share with God's _____ who are in _____.

Heb. 10:24 — Let us _____ how we may _____ one another on toward _____ and _____.

Eph. 2:10 — Just as you share in our _____, so also you share in our _____.

ANGELS OF MERCY

This table centerpiece is filled with ways to serve family members with hope and love!

Whatcha need:
- acrylic paints for pottery (black, pink)
- shiny tinsel or foil
- glue & scissors
- 4-inch clay pot
- pen or pencil
- slips of paper
- large paper doily

Whatcha do:
(1) Paint a cute face on a clay pot. (2) Cut the doily in half and glue the halves to the back of the pot for wings. (3) Glue shiny garland, tinsel, or foil to the rim of the pot. (4) Write ways to serve, help, and encourage family members on slips of paper and place them in the pot. (5) Let family members draw out papers and do what's written on them.

Fill-'em-In

Write **HEBREWS 6:19** on the spaces below, then fill those words in the puzzle.

__ __ __ __ __ __ __ __ __ __

__ __ __ __ __ __ __ __ __

__ __ __ __ __ __ __ , __ __ __ __

__ __ __ __ __ __ __ __ __ __ .

© 2001 by Susan L. Lingo.
Permission is granted to reproduce this page for ministry purposes only—not for resale.

87

Section 3 Hope for Tod

WHIZ QUIZ

Draw a line to the word that completes each sentence.

- Praying and having _____ strengthen hope. God's
- We all have difficult _____ . serving
- _____ love never fails us. Word
- _____ others spreads hope. patience
- We find hope in God's _____ . salvation
- Jesus' _____ brings us hope and joy! times

Scripture Swirl

Write the words to the **MIGHTY MEMORY VERSE** around the swirl. Use the words in the box below, if needed.

hope	this
as	for
secure	firm
and	Hebrews
have	an
soul	the
6	19
anchor	

we

88

© 2001 by Susan L. Lingo.
Permission is granted to reproduce this page for ministry purposes only—not for resale.

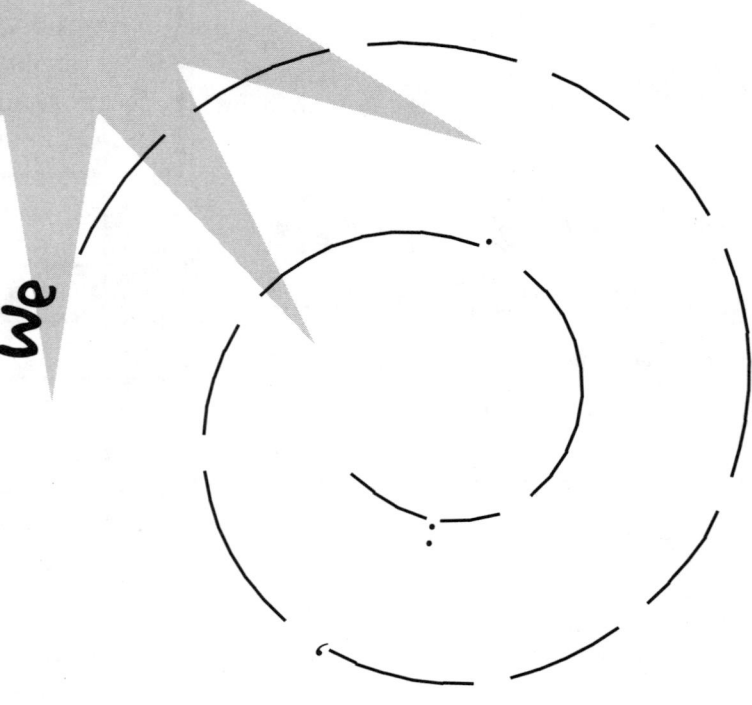

Section 4

THE ASSURANCE OF HOPE

Let us hold unswervingly
to the hope we profess,
for he who promised
is faithful.
Hebrews 10:23

Lesson 10

IT'S A SURE THING!

We have the Lord's assurance of everlasting hope.

Psalm 71:14
Jeremiah 31:17
Micah 7:7
Hebrews 11:1
1 Peter 1:3, 4

SESSION SUPPLIES

- Bibles
- brown paper sack
- small treats
- balloons
- a straight pin
- a rock and a feather
- permanent markers
- ½-inch-wide ribbon
- scissors & tape
- newsprint
- photocopies of Hebrews 10:23 (page 127)
- photocopies of the Power Page! (page 97)

MIGHTY MEMORY VERSE

Let us hold unswervingly to the hope we profess, for he who promised is faithful. Hebrews 10:23

SESSION OBJECTIVES

During this session, children will
★ discover what *assurance* means
★ understand that we can trust God's promises
★ realize that we have the assurance of hope through God's promises
★ explore how heavenly assurance goes beyond worldly hope

BIBLE BACKGROUND

We've all heard the old saying that "the only sure thing is change." But when it comes to God and having hope in his heavenly promises, the only sure thing is *no* change! God's promises are his Word and his loving assurance to us that all things he promised will be kept. In Jeremiah 31:17, God himself says, "So there is hope for your future." And in Isaiah 49:23 God says, "Then you will know that I am the LORD; those who hope in me will not be disappointed." Words like *is* and *will know* are words of assurance, and when they're spoken by the Most High we have loving assurance of heavenly insurance! When God says we will have hope for a future and will not be disappointed, we can count on it!

Lesson 10

Kids understand what being sure of something means. But the word *assurance* is probably not in their working vocabularies yet. Being sure it won't rain is different from having God's assurance of eternal life. One is an earthly certainty, while the other is a spiritual guarantee straight from God. Use this lively lesson to help kids realize that we can go beyond hope to God's supreme assurance for a future we won't be disappointed in!

POWER FOCUS

Before class, gather a small rock, a feather, a balloon, small treats (such as small erasers or wrapped candies), a straight pin, and a brown paper sack. Place the wrapped treats in the paper sack and inflate the balloon. Set the balloon and pin, rock, feather, and sack with treats on the floor.

Welcome kids and gather them around the items on the floor. Invite a volunteer to hold the rock and feather and ask kids to tell what will happen if both are dropped, such as "the rock will hit the floor first" or "the feather will float, and the rock will drop." Drop the rock and feather and see if the predictions are correct. Next, have a child hold the balloon and pin and ask what will happen if the pin is stuck into the balloon. Poke the balloon with the pin and see if the predictions are correct. Then ask:

★ **Did you *hope* or *know* what would happen with the rock and feather? the balloon and pin? Explain.**

★ **What's the difference between hoping for something to happen and knowing it will happen?**

Say: **We knew what would happen with the rock and feather and with the balloon and pin because of our prior experiences. You've probably dropped heavy and light items and watched what happened. Or maybe you've popped a balloon before with something sharp. We know things because of what we've observed or learned. When we see God's love and how he keeps his promises, we have assurance in God's power. Assurance means knowing.**

Hold up the paper sack and ask: **What do you think or hope is inside of this sack?** Allow kids time to respond, then say: **Since you didn't see what I placed inside, you really don't know for certain, but you can hope it's something really good. When we think of hope promised by God, we have his assurance that it's good! Today we'll discover more about the assurance of hope and how God's promises for our future will be kept. We'll learn a new Mighty Memory Verse about holding on to the hope**

Lesson 10

God promised us, and we'll open our sack later to see if what you hoped for is inside. Right now, let's learn the difference between everyday hopes and heavenly hope.

THE MIGHTY MESSAGE

Before class, write "heavenly hope" and "everyday hope" on two sheets of newsprint. Tape the papers to opposite walls in the room. Write the words to the Hope Rap from this activity on newsprint and tape it to a third wall or door.

Gather kids in the center of the room and say: **When most people in the wold think of the word *hope*, they think of what they would like to see happen. For example, if someone says, "I hope it doesn't rain for our picnic," that person isn't sure if it will rain or not but hopes it will stay dry. We can think of this kind of worldly hope as "everyday hope."** (Point to the sign that says "everyday hope.")

Everyday hopes are good, but sometimes they disappoint us. After all, it might rain for that picnic! But with God and his promises, we have a different kind of hope that never disappoints us. When we know, love, and follow God and trust his promises, we have "heavenly hope" and the assurance that God will do what he has promised! (Point to the sign that says "heavenly hope.") **Isn't that neat? We have the assurance of heavenly hope that comes only from God and is powerful enough to defeat any doubts, fears, or worries.**

Let's see if you can tell the difference between everyday hopes that sometimes disappoint us and heavenly hope that never disappoints us because it's from God. I'll read some hope sentences. If you think the hope is everyday hope that could disappoint us, run and stand beside the sign that says "everyday hope." If the hope is a heavenly hope from God and can't disappoint us, run and stand beside the sign that says "heavenly hope."

Read the following sentences and wait for kids to choose a sign to run to. Then ask kids to briefly tell why they made each choice.

POWER POINTERS

Make a list of assurances God gives us, such as the assurance of his love, the certainty of his answers to prayer, and the surety of his nearness.

Lesson 10

★ I hope it snows for Christmas. (everyday hope)
★ I hope God will help me. (heavenly hope)
★ I hope Mom bakes cookies today! (everyday hope)
★ I hope my friend can play today. (everyday hope)
★ I hope God will stay with me. (heavenly hope)
★ I hope God hears my prayers. (heavenly hope)
★ I hope we have spaghetti for dinner. (everyday hope)
★ I hope Jesus saves a place for me in heaven. (heavenly hope)

Have kids sit in place as you read aloud Micah 7:7; Jeremiah 31:17a; Hebrews 11:1; and 1 Peter 1:3, 4. Then ask:

★ Why is it good to have everyday hopes? Why is it more important to have heavenly hope?
★ How is heavenly hope more powerful than everyday hopes?
★ Why do we know heavenly hope won't ever disappoint us?

Say: **It's fine, good, and helpful to have everyday hopes. But when everyday hopes fail us, we know heavenly hope will not! Because we know, love, and follow God, we can claim heavenly hope for our own and never be truly hopeless. God promised to help us, love us, stay near us, and give us eternal life when we love and accept Jesus. And we have the assurance that those hopes will never fail or disappoint us. Wow! That makes me feel great! Let's express our joy at having the assurance of heavenly hope by rapping out a new Hope Rap.**

Lead kids in the Hope Rap by reading the words in rhythm and clapping. Have kids make up moves to accompany the verses and chorus.

HOPE RAP

Some people hope the rains will fall;
Others hope their friends might call—
Some people put their hope in money,
But that kinda hope will fail you, honey!

(chorus) So I put my hopes far up above me,
In my God who knows and loves me!
For what God has promised will come true,
And heavenly hope won't disappoint you!

Some people hope they'll pass the test,
Others hope they'll find some rest—

Lesson 10

Some people put their hope in "rabbit-foots,"
But that kinda hope will fail you, toots!
   (Repeat chorus)

Say: That was a neat rap with a powerful reminder that heavenly hope won't disappoint us. Now let's see how walking a straight path in hope can help us.

THE MESSAGE IN MOTION

Before class, cut a 10-foot length of ribbon and tape the ends in a straight line across the floor. Next, tape a squiggly ribbon line to the floor beginning and ending at the ends of the straight ribbon.

Form two teams: the straight-liners and the swervy-liners. Have teams line up at the same end of the ribbons. Explain that in this relay, one player from each team will walk heel-to-toe along their team's line: one in a straight path and one in a swervy fashion to the opposite ends of the ribbons. Then the next players in line can travel the ribbons. The relay will continue until one team's players have completed walking the ribbon. (Of course, the straight-line team should finish first because it has less ribbon to cover!)

When the relay is over, ask:

★ Why did the straight-line team reach their goal more quickly than the swervy-liners?

★ In what ways is this relay like having hope that focuses on God and doesn't swerve or wiggle around?

Say: When we have hope that goes directly to God, it's hope that helps us reach our goal of trusting God and getting through the rough path of life we travel. Some people, just as our rap said, put their hope in different things and swerve from one object of hope to another— and they're usually disappointed! But when we hold unswervingly to the hope we have in the Lord, it's a straight, sure hope that leads us to our goal, who is God! Our new Mighty Memory Verse teaches us more about holding unswervingly to the hope we have in God. Let's add the words to our new Mighty Memory Verse to our game setup.

Lesson 10

SUPER SCRIPTURE

Before class, write the following words or groups of words on strips of newsprint and tape them in place on the straight ribbon as in the illustration: "Let us hold" (strip 1), "unswervingly" (strip 2), "to the hope" (strip 3), "we profess" (strip 4), "for he who promised is faithful. Hebrews 10:23" (strip 5). Write the entire verse (Hebrews 10:23) on another sheet of newsprint.

Have kids stand beside the words "Let us hold." Lead kids in walking beside the words as they repeat them aloud. Let pairs of kids walk the line as they repeat Hebrews 10:23. Then say: **We just discovered that it's important to not swerve in our hope but to focus our hope on God. When we hold unswervingly to the hope we profess or believe, we find assurance in God's promises. Why? Because he who promised is faithful. In other words, God promised us hope, and he always keeps his promises!**

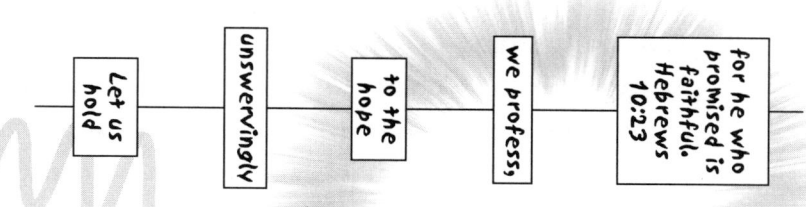

Hold up the newsprint paper with Hebrews 10:23 written on it and have kids repeat the Mighty Memory Verse two more times. If there's time, let pairs walk the ribbon line again as they repeat the verse.

Say: **Remember how our sack represents the goodness of God's promises and the hope we have in those promises? After learning about holding on to hope because God is faithful, you ought to be able to tell me if you *hope* something good is in here or have *assurance* that there's something good inside.** Have kids tell that they *know* it must be good because it represents God's promises, which are always good. Then open the sack and let kids enjoy the treats.

Read aloud Psalm 71:14. Say: **Let's praise God with a prayer thanking him for our assurance of hope and for keeping his promises.** Keep the verse on newsprint to use next week.

A POWERFUL PROMISE

Before class, make copies of the Scripture Strip for Hebrews 10:23 (page 127). Hand each child a balloon to blow up and tie off. Then cut the ribbon

95

Lesson 10

from the game setup into streamers and let kids tie the streamers to their balloons. Tape a Scripture strip for Hebrews 10:23 to each ribbon, then have kids use permanent markers to write "Hope: It's a Sure Thing!" on their balloons.

As kids work, say: **We've learned today that assurance means *knowing* something will happen and that we have assurance of hope when we love God. We've learned that there's everyday hope, which often disappoints us, and that we have a special heavenly hope that can never disappoint us. And we've started learning a new Mighty Memory Verse.** Have kids read Hebrews 10:23 from their Scripture strips.

Say: **God has made us many wonderful promises, such as being with us, hearing our prayers, helping us, and offering us eternal life through Jesus. We can make our own promises to God to hold unswervingly to the hope we have in him.** Have kids hold their praise balloons as you pray: **Dear Lord, we thank you for heavenly hope that never disappoints us. We thank you for your promises you always keep. And we ask for your help in holding on to the hope you have given us through your power and love. Amen.**

Lead kids in rapping the Hope Rap as they wave and gently bounce their balloons in time to the rhythm. Then read aloud Psalm 71:14 and end with this responsive good-bye:

Leader: **May you always hold on to God's hope.**

Children: **And also you!**

Distribute the Power Page! take-home papers as kids are leaving. Thank children for coming and encourage them to keep their promises of holding on to God's hope this week.

Lesson 10

POWER PAGE!

The Assurance of Hope

A Sure Thing!

Fill in the spaces below. The circled letters spell out the wonderful gift God promises us!

- month after July ○ _ _ _ _ _
- opposite of go ○ _ _ _
- a stinky animal ○ _ _ _ _
- opposite of over ○ _ _ _ _
- color of apples ○ _ _
- tiny insect ○ _ _
- opposite of always ○ _ _ _ _
- "moo" animal ○ _ _
- what hens lay ○ _ _ _

of

- Valentine symbol ○ _ _ _ _
- opposite of new ○ _ _
- opposite of push ○ _ _ _
- not hard ○ _ _ _

HEAVENLY OR EVERYDAY?

Everyday hope sometimes disappoints us, but heavenly hope never does! Draw matching lines to tell if each hope is everyday or heavenly.

I hope it doesn't rain.	Heavenly hope
I hope God answers me.	Heavenly hope
I hope God loves me.	Everyday hope
I hope lunch is soon.	Heavenly hope
I hope I get a new bike.	Everyday hope
I hope God is with me.	Everyday hope

Hope does not disappoint us, because God has poured out his love into our hearts. Romans 5:5

High & Low

Fill in the missing high, low, and in-between letters to complete Hebrews 10:23.

© 2001 by Susan L. Lingo.
Permission is granted to reproduce this page for ministry purposes only—not for resale.

97

Lesson 11

A LIGHT IN DARKNESS

Hope in the Lord lights our darkest days.

Romans 4:18-24
2 Corinthians 4:4, 6-9
2 Timothy 3:12

SESSION SUPPLIES

★ Bibles
★ matches & a candle
★ a lamp & flashlight
★ a picture of the sun
★ sheets of star stickers
★ scissors & markers
★ index cards
★ self-hardening clay
★ tea-light candles
★ toothpicks or bobby pins
★ photocopies of the Power Page! (page 105)

MIGHTY MEMORY VERSE

Let us hold unswervingly to the hope we profess, for he who promised is faithful. Hebrews 10:23

(For older kids who need a challenge, also work on learning Hebrews 11:1: "Now faith is being sure of what we hope for and certain of what we do not see.")

SESSION OBJECTIVES

During this session, children will
★ understand that we all go through tough times
★ realize that Satan tries to steal our hope
★ discover that the Lord's love shines hope into our lives
★ explore how hope carries us through dark days

BIBLE BACKGROUND

How many times have you asked, "Why me?" when things go awry? When we're in the throes of frustrations, struggles, and discouragement, we often forget that all of us go through times that are dark and disappointing, hard and seemingly hopeless. The Bible calls these times "trials and tribulations." And though we all share the common bond of dark days, Christians also share another bond—one of glorious love and assurance that lights our darkest days with hope. Paul reminds us in 2 Corinthians 4:6 that God shone his light into our hearts so we would know his glory and receive the hope that he freely offers. So take heart the next time your days seem dark or despairing, for no darkness can prevail against the bright hope God gives us!

Kids often forget to see the rainbow through the rain or bright stars in the dark of night. But it's important they realize that hard times are a part of life just as much as bright hope is a part of knowing and loving the Lord. Use this lesson to help kids understand that our dark days aren't as dark as they believe, that these times are lit by the hope that only God can light and ignite in our hearts.

POWER focus

Before class, collect matches, a candle, a flashlight, a lamp or a bright shop light, and a picture of the sun. You'll be comparing the strength of light from these items.

Place the light sources in a pile beside you. Welcome kids to class and gather them around the items. Light the match and hold it up as you say: **This match gives off a little bit of light, but not for long!** Use the match to light the candle, then blow out the match. Say: **This candle gives more light than the match. It's a stronger light, but still not very bright.**

Blow out the candle and have kids order the remaining lights in the order of their strength (the flashlight, the lamp or shop light, and the sun). Then ask:

★ **If you were in darkness, which light would you choose to shine on you? Explain.**

★ **How does light help us see more clearly?**

★ **In what ways is hope from God like a bright light in our lives?**

Say: **When days seem dark because of worries, fears, sadness, or doubt, we might feel hopeless. But the light of God's power and love shines hope into our lives and helps us see more clearly. We see that, with God on our side, things aren't really so dark after all.**

Today we'll discover how hope from the Lord is like a bright light or beacon that shines over us. We'll see how Satan tries to steal that light from us and how he wants to steal away our hope. And we'll explore how we can keep the light of hope shining in even the darkest of times when things might seem impossible. But first, let's discover how Abraham found hope in what seemed like an impossible situation.

Lesson 11

THE MIGHTY MESSAGE

Before class, cut apart the stars on several sheets of stickers but leave the backing paper on. (Cut between the rows of stars for speedy snipping!) You'll need as many stars as you can snip. Kids will have the seemingly impossible job of counting the stars but will discover they can count them in teams quickly.

Have kids sit in a circle, then place the stars in a big pile. Ask kids if they think they can count the stars in a minute (two minutes if you have young children). Then form six teams and give each team a pile to count.

After one or two minutes, tally up the counts and announce the number of stars. Then say: **It seemed impossible to count all those stars so quickly, didn't it? Abraham had an impossible situation too—or he** thought **it was impossible. Let's see how hope and God's power changed the impossible to the possible for Abraham.**

Abraham loved God with all his heart but was sad because he had no children. The situation seemed totally hopeless. He was very old, and so was his wife Sarah. They were both close to 100 years old—too old to have kids! But God spoke to Abraham one night and told him to look at the stars.

Gently toss the pile of stars in the center of the circle. Say: **God promised Abraham he would have children and told Abraham he would make a great nation that numbered as many as the stars in the sky! Now to most people, that would seem a hopeless thing, since Abraham and Sarah were so old. But is anything impossible with God? Never! Let's see what happened next.**

Invite volunteers to read aloud Romans 4:18-24. Then ask:

★ **Why did Abraham have hope even though the situation seemed hopeless?**

★ **In what ways did Abraham's hope strengthen his faith?**

★ **Why did God honor Abraham's hope and faith?**

Say: **Abraham didn't waver or swerve in his hope. In fact, we're told that Abraham's hope strengthened his faith in God's power! And**

POWER POINTERS

Kids might enjoy painting their own cool light bulbs. Use heat-resistant paints from craft stores and paint the glass portion of 40-watt bulbs. After they're dry, use them in lamps without the shades.

Lesson 11

because Abraham had faith and hope, God gave Abraham the children he promised! God honored Abraham for having hope in the darkest of times, and God will honor our hope too. We all have tough times when situations seem impossible. That's part of life. But when we have heavenly hope and faith in God, God will shine his help, love, and power into our lives just as he did with Abraham.

Hand each child three index cards to cut in half. Let kids put star stickers on the cards, then write any fears, doubts, worries, or "impossible" situations they need hope for on the cards. (If there are blank cards, have kids keep them to use later.)

Say: **Your challenge is to remain hopeful over these situations, knowing that God can and will offer his help just as he helped Abraham.** Read aloud Hebrews 11:1. Say: **Remember what Hebrews 11:1 teaches us, that faith is the *assurance* of things hoped for and being sure of what we can't see. In other words, we need to trust God for hope and help in all situations. Now let's learn more about the heavenly hope that shines in our hearts.**

THE MESSAGE IN MOTION

Before class, purchase self-hardening clay at a craft department or art supply store. Self-hardening clay air dries in several hours. If you choose to use regular clay, send a brief note home telling parents to wait one week before lighting the tea light candles inside.

Say: **There's a wonderful Bible passage that tells us about being jars of clay with a special treasure of great hope inside. It also reminds us of the light of hope we have in Jesus.** Invite volunteers to read aloud 2 Corinthians 4:4, 6-9. Then say: **Because we often have tough times that seem dark and sad, we might feel hopeless. But these verses remind us that Jesus shines a great light of hope into our hearts and lives. And even though we're fragile, like jars of clay, the Lord's hope is like**

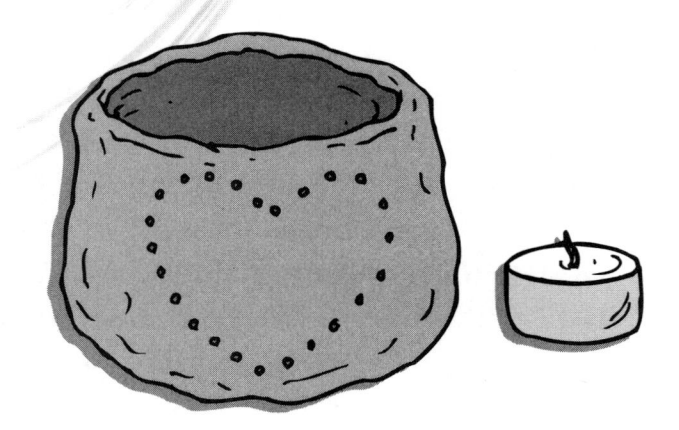

101

Lesson 11

a treasure inside us that comes from God and nowhere else. Let's make jars-of-clay candleholders to remind us of the light of the Lord's hope that shines within us.

Hand each child a lump of clay about the size of a tennis ball. Show kids how to work the clay into smooth balls. Then demonstrate how to poke thumbs down into the centers of the clay balls and gently pinch the sides around and up to make pinch pots. Be sure the sides are about ¼-inch thick. When the clay jars are formed, have kids use toothpicks or bobby pins to carefully poke holes in the sides.

Explain that the holes will shine light out through the jars when small candles are lit inside. Finally, hand each child a tea light to place inside the clay jar. Tell kids to have an adult light their candles but not until the clay is hard and dry.

Say: **We may be fragile humans, like jars of clay, but we have the love, power, help, and hope of God to make us strong! And this strength helps us hold on to hope. Let's review our Mighty Memory Verse that teaches us about holding on unswervingly to our heavenly hope.** Set the pots aside to dry.

SUPER SCRIPTURE

Be sure the newsprint verse for Hebrews 10:23 is still on the wall for kids to read.

Have kids repeat Hebrews 10:23 three times aloud, then challenge pairs of kids to repeat the verse without peeking. Hand out the remaining star stickers when the verse is repeated by the pairs.

Say: **Last week we learned what *unswervingly* means. It means that we keep God as our focus and follow the straight line that he shows us. And when we hold on to hope unswervingly, we have the assurance that this hope will never disappoints us.** Ask:

★ **How does knowing that God is faithful help us hold on to hope?**

★ **In what ways does professing or telling others about our hope in God help us hold on to hope?**

Say: **When we speak hopefully, have faith in God's power, and hope only in God, we're able to hold unswervingly to hope. That's wonderful, isn't it? But Satan doesn't like us to have such strong hope.** Read 2 Timothy 3:12, then say: **Satan would like nothing better than to steal our hope away and fill us with doubts and fears. It's important to hold**

Lesson 11

on to the hope God freely gives us by speaking hopeful words, praying, and focusing on God. This Mighty Memory Verse is a good one to repeat whenever you need an extra boost of "holding-on-to" power! We can also sing the Hope Rap to remind us that the hope we find in God never disappoints us.

Lead kids in rapping the Hope Rap from last week. If you have the words from last week, tape them to the wall for kids to read.

HOPE RAP

Some people hope the rains will fall;
Others hope their friends might call—
Some people put their hope in money,
But that kinda hope will fail you, honey!

(chorus) So I put my hopes far up above me,
In my God who knows and loves me!
For what God has promised will come true,
And heavenly hope won't disappoint you!

Some people hope they'll pass the test,
Others hope they'll find some rest—
Some people put their hope in "rabbit-foots,"
But that kinda hope will fail you, toots!
(Repeat chorus)

After rapping, say: **Wow! Having hope makes me feel strong and thankful. Let's thank God with a prayer for giving us hope that shines light into our lives every day.** Keep the newsprint verse to use next week.

A POWERFUL PROMISE

Gather kids and have them hold the index cards they prepared earlier. Say: **We've been learning so much about the power of hope and the powerful**

103

Lesson 11

hope we hold on to. Today we discovered that having troubles is to be expected but that God shines hope into the dark times. We learned that Satan tries to steal away our hope and that we must hold unswervingly to the hope we have in the Lord. Finally, we reviewed our Mighty Memory Verse that says (lead kids in repeating Hebrews 10:23). (If you have older kids, introduce Hebrews 11:1 at this time.)

Then say: **You have cards on which you've written doubts, fears, or situations that seem impossible. Let's offer a prayer of thanks to God. When we get to the part about asking for his help, you can silently read your cards.** Pray: **Dear Lord, we thank you for the bright hope you shine into our lives. Please show us ways to hold on to the hope you offer. And Lord, please give us hope for these situations.** (Pause as kids silently read their cards). **We're so glad the hope we have in you never disappoints us, Lord. Amen.**

End with this responsive good-bye:

Leader: **May the hope you find in God be with you.**

Children: **And also with you!**

Distribute the Power Page! take-home papers as kids are leaving. Thank children for coming and encourage them to keep their hope in God strong this week.

Lesson 11

The Assurance of Hope

POWER PAGE!

LIGHTS OF L♥VE!

Draw four things that give light, then use your Bible to complete the verse.

"For ____, who said, 'Let _____ _____ out of darkness,' made his _____ _____ in our _____ to give us the _____ of the knowledge of the _____ of God in the face of _____." 2 Corinthians 4:6

LEMON DE-LIGHTS

Make these light 'n tasty delights to remind your family and friends of the light of God's love!

Whatcha need:
- ♥ a package of refrigerator cookie dough
- ♥ canned lemon icing
- ♥ bowl
- ♥ cookie sheet
- ♥ cheese grater
- ♥ fresh lemon

Whatcha do: 
(1) Flatten dough to ¼-inch thick. (2) Cut out ♥-shaped cookies and place them on a cookie sheet. (3) Bake according to package directions, then cool. (4) Place icing in a bowl and squeeze in 1 tablespoon of freshly squeezed lemon juice. (5) Frost cookies, then sprinkle with grated lemon rind.

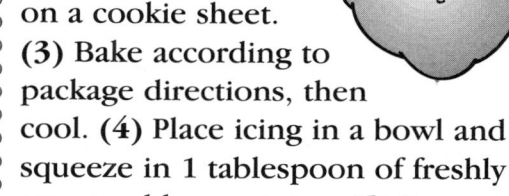

LETTER BEFORE

Write the letter that comes before the letter under each space to complete Hebrews 10:23.

___ ___ ___   ___ ___   ___ ___ ___ ___   ___ ___ ___ ___ ___ ___ ___ ___ ___ ___   ___ ___
M F U   V T   I P M E   V O T X F S W J O H M Z   U P

___ ___ ___   ___ ___ ___ ___   ___ ___   ___ ___ ___ ___ ___ ___ ___,   ___ ___ ___   ___ ___   ___ ___ ___
U I F   I P Q F   X F   Q S P G F T T,   G P S   I F   X I P

___ ___ ___ ___ ___ ___ ___ ___   ___ ___   ___ ___ ___ ___ ___ ___ ___ ___.
Q S P N J T F E   J T   G B J U I G V M

© 2001 by Susan L. Lingo.
Permission is granted to reproduce this page for ministry purposes only—not for resale.

105

Lesson 12

TARGET: HOPE!

Patience and perseverance help us hold on to hope.

Psalms 27:14; 33:20, 21; 130:5
Romans 5:3-5
Jude 21

SESSION SUPPLIES

- ★ Bibles
- ★ permanent markers & crayons
- ★ 4 balloons
- ★ scissors & tape
- ★ poster board
- ★ round cardboard pizza trays
- ★ metal washers
- ★ photocopies of the Right On Target verses (page 125)
- ★ photocopies of the Whiz Quiz (page 114) and the Power Page! (page 113)

MIGHTY MEMORY VERSE

Let us hold unswervingly to the hope we profess, for he who promised is faithful. Hebrews 10:23
(For older kids who need a challenge, also work on learning Hebrews 11:1: "Now faith is being sure of what we hope for and certain of what we do not see.")

SESSION OBJECTIVES

During this session, children will
★ realize that patience and perseverance strengthen hope
★ understand that God works in his own time and way
★ learn that hope means never giving up
★ discover that hope can come from suffering

BIBLE BACKGROUND

What's the toughest thing for modern people to do? Wait! With the hurry-up world of quick cars, fast-food meals, accelerated computer power, and instant messaging, patience is not only a rare virtue, it's nearly vanished! With this mega-fast mentality, we find it nearly impossible to wait on lunch, let alone on God. If we're sad, we want a quick smile. If we're frustrated, we desire a rapid resolution. And if we feel hopeless, we demand a speedy solution. But Psalm 33:20, 21 reminds us that our job is to wait on God and trust his timing and answers. Hope, then, often depends on our level of patience and perseverance. When we have faith in God

Lesson 12

and his power, we're able to wait for his help with sanguine assurance and optimistic patience.

Kids and patience? There couldn't be a more contradictory pair of words! Lively and spontaneous, impulsive and impetuous, most kids race forward in a headlong fashion without much thought of patience or perseverance. But the Bible doesn't call patience a fruit of the Spirit lightly! Patience and never giving up are key components in faith and following God with obedience and humility. Patience and perseverance also strengthen hope as we wait for God's intervention. Use this lesson to teach kids that waiting on the Lord and never giving up hope are what God calls us to do in trying times.

POWER FOCUS

Before class, be sure you have a chair for every two kids.

Welcome kids to class and let them know you're glad they are in class. Say: **Find a partner and let's see how much perseverance and patience you have!** Tell kids to decide which partner will be the holder and which will be the helper. Have each holder place a chair in front of her. Explain that in this activity, the holders will hold the chairs at arm's length for as long as they're able. When they feel they need relief, they can call in their helpers to help hold the chairs. Tell kids you'll call time at the end of four minutes to see which pairs are still holding chairs. If you have time, have kids switch roles and repeat this activity so everyone has a turn being both a holder and a helper.

After you call time, set the chairs down. Say: **Wow! That activity took a great deal of patience and perseverance, didn't it?** Ask:

★ **How did it feel to hold the chairs without help?**

★ **In what ways did it help to call in a helper for relief?**

★ **How did it help your patience and perseverance to know there was help waiting?**

Say: **Holding up those chairs was a bit like holding on to heavy troubles, worries, or other sufferings. But knowing you had help just a heartbeat away helped you have perseverance and hope. That's just how it is when we have hard and heavy situations in life but know that help is near with the Lord! When we have patience and perseverance and wait on the Lord, our hope becomes stronger.**

Today we'll discover how patience and perseverance help us stay on target for hope. We'll learn that God helps us in his time and in his way

Lesson 12

and that our job is to have hope and wait. And we'll review our Mighty Memory Verse that teaches to hold unswervingly on to hope. Right now, let's explore how patience and perseverance help strengthen our hope.

THE MIGHTY MESSAGE

Before class, inflate four balloons and write the following words on the balloons, one word per balloon: *sufferings, perseverance, character, hope.* You'll also need four 3-by-6-inch strips of poster board and one 8-inch poster-board circle. Draw thick arrows across three of the strips and a thick equals sign (=) on the fourth strip. Write the word "disappoint" on the circle shape, then draw a slash line diagonally through the word to signify "no disappointment." Have tape handy for later in the activity.

Have kids stand in a close circle. Hold the balloons and say: **We'll use these balloons to help us discover how patience and perseverance help strengthen hope. Who can read the words on the balloons for us?**

Invite volunteers to read aloud the words in the following order: sufferings, perseverance, character, and hope. Ask kids what each word means. Then say: **As we read some wonderful verses from the Bible, we'll bop and juggle these balloons back and forth around the circle. See if you can keep the balloons moving without letting them touch the floor.**

Read aloud the following from Romans 5:3-5: **We also rejoice in our sufferings ...** (start bopping the balloon with "sufferings" written on it around the circle). After a few moments, continue: **Because we know that suffering produces perseverance ...** (add the balloon with "perseverance" written on it), **perseverance produces character ...** (add in the balloon with "character" written on it), **character produces hope** (add in the balloon with "hope" written on it). Continue: **And hope does not disappoint us, because God has poured out his love into our hearts by the Holy Spirit, whom he has given us.**

Continue bopping the balloons as you say: **You see? Strong hope actually comes from suffering and going through tough times! The Bible tells**

POWER POINTERS

Give kids tools for waiting on God by brainstorming things to do as you wait. Suggestions might include praying, reading the Bible, talking to a friend or someone at church, or writing God a letter.

108

Lesson 12

us that suffering leads to perseverance, then character, then hope—and hope never disappoints us! Freeze and hold the balloons.

Pause, then continue: **Now let's review how hope is made strong. Which comes first?** Have the child holding the "sufferings" balloon read it aloud, then tape it to the wall so it can be read. Continue in the same way through perseverance, character, and hope. (Leave enough room between the balloons for the poster-board strips that you'll add in a moment.)

When the balloons are taped to the wall in order from left to right, ask kids the following questions:

★ **How do suffering and going through hard times and experiences help us have patience?**

★ **Why is perseverance a good character trait to have? How does it help us have hope?**

Say: **Isn't it strange? When we have hard times and still have patience and perseverance through them, it actually strengthens our hope instead of destroying it! God works things in such amazing ways, doesn't he? God knows when we have hard times, but he lets us go through them to teach us about having perseverance and hope—and to teach us to wait on him. God does bring help, but in his time and in his way. It's our job to hold on to hope and wait for the Lord.**

Read aloud Psalms 27:14 and 33:20, 21. Then have kids read the words on the balloons. Tape the poster-board arrows between the words *sufferings* and *perseverance, perseverance* and *character,* and *character* and *hope.* Finally, tape the equals sign after *hope* and add the "no disappointment" circle. Invite kids to take turns reading your Scripture "equation" as follows: "Sufferings lead to perseverance; perseverance leads to character; character leads to hope; and hope never disappoints us."

Say: **This Scripture equation is right on target for teaching us how to strengthen hope. Now let's make special targets to use in a game and**

109

Lesson 12

to remind us that having patience and perseverance are right on target for strong hope.

THE MESSAGE IN MOTION

Before class, collect clean, 12-inch (or larger) cardboard pizza rounds from a pizza shop. (These are the cardboard trays that come under pizzas.) If you can't find ready-made rounds, cut your own 12-inch circles from cardboard or poster board. Photocopy the Right On Target verse boxes (page 125), one set for each child. Cut circle patterns from poster board as follows: a 4-inch circle, a 6-inch circle, an 8-inch circle, and a 10-inch circle. Be sure you have a metal washer for each child. You may wish to make a Right On Target game board as a sample for kids to follow.

Distribute the pizza rounds and metal washers. Have kids put their initials on the washers. (These will be used later to toss onto the game boards.) Have kids trace circles on their pizza rounds, smallest to largest, so they look like targets. Using crayons, color every other circle red. In tiny letters on the smallest circle, use markers to write "#1-sufferings." On the next circle, write "#2-perseverance." Next, write "#3-character." And on the last circle, write "#4-hope." Finally, tape the Right On Target verse boxes around the edge of the game board.

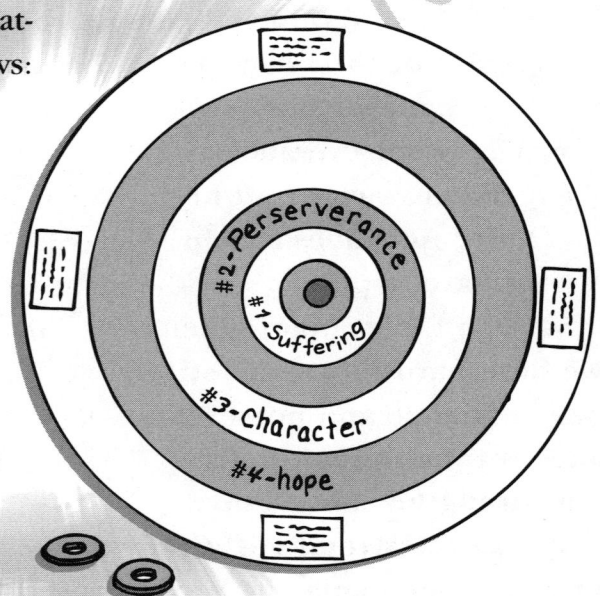

When the game boards are done, have kids get with partners and place the target game boards about three feet apart. Have partners take turns tossing the metal washers onto the targets. Whichever circle the washer lands on, score that many points and read the corresponding verse box. For example, if a washer lands on "#2-perseverance," score two points and read verse box #2. After five tosses from each partner, total the scores. End by having partners give each other high fives.

Say: **Wow! Strengthening our hope is like a giant, spiritual target with rings that grow bigger. We go from suffering to perseverance to**

110

Lesson 12

character to hope—and we're never disappointed in hope! That's because God sends us his hope through love and through the Holy Spirit, who helps us wait on the Lord. That works out neatly, doesn't it? So the next time you have hard times, have patience and perseverance as you wait on the Lord to help. Your hope will be stronger, and God will honor your patience! Let's see how holding unswervingly to hope helps us through tough times, just as an arrow travels unswervingly to a target.

SUPER SCRIPTURE

Cut the newsprint from last week with Hebrews 10:23 written on it into as many pieces as there are kids in class.

Hand each child a piece of the verse. Repeat Hebrews 10:23 three times aloud, then challenge kids to reassemble the verse without talking. When the verse is complete, have kids give each other high fives for their great teamwork. (If kids are working on the extra-challenge verse, do the same with Hebrews 11:1.) Then say: **It took patience and perseverance to put our Scripture puzzle together—but you stuck with it without giving up. That's what perseverance means.** Ask:

★ **How does holding on to hope without giving up help us through hard situations?**

★ **Why do you think God wants us to have hope without giving up?**

★ **What trouble or hard situation can you persevere through this week as you hold on to hope?**

Say: **It's not always easy to wait on the Lord. God will help us and answer prayers, but he does it in his time and in his way. It's up to us to trust in God and in his promises. And it's up to us to hold on to hope without giving up no matter how hard that might be. God will honor us when we have perseverance and patience and hold on to hope. Let's end our time by asking for God's help in persevering through tough times and holding on to the hope he gives us.**

A POWERFUL PROMISE

Gather kids and say: **What a lot we've learned today! We've discovered that suffering isn't always bad—that it builds character and perseverance, which strengthens hope. We've learned that it's important to wait**

Lesson 12

on the Lord for him to send help in his time and way. And we've explored how having patience and perseverance keeps us right on target for having strong hope without giving up.

Hold up the Bible and say: **God's Word teaches us about holding on to hope and trusting in God's promises. We can promise to seek God's help in waiting on him and having hope no matter how hard the situation. We'll pass the Bible around the circle. As you hold the Bible, say, "Lord, help me call on you in patience and hope."**

When everyone has had a turn to hold the Bible, close with a prayer asking for God's help in having patience, perseverance, and strong hope. End with a corporate "amen."

Before kids leave, allow five or ten minutes to complete the Whiz Quiz. If you run out of time, be sure to complete this page first thing next week. The Whiz Quiz is an invaluable tool that allows kids, teachers, and parents see what kids have learned in the previous three weeks.

Close by reading aloud Jude 21, then end with this responsive good-bye:

Leader: **May you always wait on the Lord with patience and hope.**
Children: **And also you!**

Distribute the Power Page! take-home papers as kids are leaving. Remind kids to take home their Right On Target game boards and encourage them to keep their promises to seek God's help, hope, and perseverance this week.

Lesson 12

The Assurance of Hope

POWER PAGE!

HOPE → COPE

Having hope from God helps us cope with tough times and get past sticky situations. Use your Bible to complete Romans 5:3b, 4a, then solve the puzzle at the bottom (Psalm 27:14) to discover how to hope in the Lord.

"__ know that __ __ __ __ __ __
 13   4 11 7 9

produces __ __ __ __ __ __ __ __ __
         2   12

__;

perseverance, __ __ __ __ __ __ __ __;
              10   1

and character, __ __ __. And hope does
                 6

not __ __ __ __ __ __ __ us."
    8 3   5

__ __ __ __ for the L __ __ __; be
13 3 7 1   6 2 8

__ __ __ __ __ and take __ __ __ __ __
4 1 2 6 5 9   10 12 3 2 1

Take Time

Make this cool "clock" to help you wait on God with patience and perseverance.

You'll need 2 plastic soft-drink bottles (same size), duct tape, several cups of sand, a jar of glitter, and glue.

Fill 1 bottle ½ to ¾ full of sand and glitter. Lay the bottle on its side and match the opening exactly with the other bottle. Duct tape the bottles together at the necks.

Use your clock like a giant egg timer or hour glass. Time on a regular clock how long it takes to empty one bottle into another. When you're feeling troubled, pray for as long as the sand takes to empty. **Remember:** God *will* hear and answer in his time!

M_SS_NG V_W_LS

Use the letters a, e, i, o, and u to complete the words to the **MIGHTY MEMORY VERSE**.

L_t _s h_ld _nsw_rv_ngly t_ th_ h_p_ w_

pr_f_ss, f_r h_ wh_ pr_m_s_d _s f_ _thf_l

H_br_ws 10:23

© 2001 by Susan L. Lingo.
Permission is granted to reproduce this page for ministry purposes only—not for resale.

113

Section 4

The Assurance of Hope

WHIZ QUIZ

Color in T (true) or F (false) to answer the following questions.

1. Assurance means being sure or knowing.   T F
2. God's Word does not give us assurance.   T F
3. Everyday hope does not disappoint us.   T F
4. God assures us of a hope and a future.   T F
5. Suffering is never of any use.   T F
6. Patience and perseverance lead to hope.   T F

AIM THE ARROWS

Draw arrows to place the words in their correct positions to complete the Mighty Memory Verse. The first word has been done for you.

us   he   we   the   profess   hope

to   Let ___ ___ ___ ___ ___   unswervingly

Let ___ ___ ___ ___ ___

hold ___ ___ ___ ___ ___   promised

for ___ ___ ___, ___ ___   10

is   faithful   who   23   Hebrews

114

© 2001 by Susan L. Lingo.
Permission is granted to reproduce this page for ministry purposes only—not for resale.

Lesson 13

REVIEW LESSON

Because of the LORD's great love we are not consumed, for his compassions never fail.
Lamentations 3:22

Lesson 13

HOPE FINDERS!

With God as our eyes and heart, we see and feel hope every day!

Isaiah 40:31; 57:10
Lamentations 3:21-23

SESSION SUPPLIES

★ Bibles
★ poster board
★ scissors, glue, & tape
★ permanent markers
★ colored vinyl tape
★ self-adhesive magnetic strip
★ adhesive picture hangers
★ used metal cookie sheets
★ two packages of cookies
★ plastic sandwich bags & twist-tie wires
★ photocopies of the Smart Cookie strip (page 120)
★ tube or canned icing & candy sprinkles
★ photocopies of the Smart Cookie Calendar (page 126)

MIGHTY MEMORY VERSE

This is a review lesson of all four Mighty Memory Verses: Psalm 31:24; Proverbs 23:18; Hebrews 6:19; and Hebrews 10:23.

SESSION OBJECTIVES

During this session, children will
★ review where hope comes from
★ understand that God's hope never disappoints us
★ learn that God gives us fresh hope each day
★ know that when we love and obey God, we're not hopeless

BIBLE BACKGROUND

Coaches know that thinking in positive terms helps team players have an edge in the game. It's no different in the game of life! Hope and a positive attitude of assurance and conviction go a long way in keeping us focused on God and his help. Just look at the positive words in the following verses: "They *will* soar on wings like eagles" (Isaiah 40:31); "his compassions *never* fail. They *are* new each morning" (Lamentations 3:22, 23); "You *will* be secure, because there *is* hope" (Job 11:18). God wants us to leave no room for doubt when it comes to heavenly hope. And the best part? Hope is made new and fresh each day of our lives!

Oftentimes kids talk themselves out of hopeful thinking and feeling just by thinking negative thoughts such as

Lesson 13

"I can't do it" or "God isn't really with me." It's vital for kids to know that assurance means being positive of what will happen and that God assures us of a future and hope each day of our lives. Use this encouraging lesson to remind kids that hope isn't a sometimes thing; it's what we have, feel, and live on a day-to-day basis when we know, love, and follow God!

POWER FOCUS

Before class, collect an old, clean metal cookie sheet for each child. Be sure the sheets aren't corroded or dented. Since this is the "grand finale" lesson of *Hope Finders,* the review project is extra fun and requires a bit more cost than average, "everyday" craft ideas. You'll need plenty of colored vinyl tape (in red, green, yellow, and blue), which can be found in hardware stores in the electrical supplies aisle. Kids will be making cool Cookie Calendars with magnetic hearts to remind them of the hope they have in the Lord each day. Later in the lesson, you'll also need self-adhesive magnetic strip and adhesive picture hangers to hang the calendars on a wall. For this activity, you'll need just the cookie sheets.

Warmly welcome kids and lead them in rapping out the Hope Rap. Encourage kids to clap and snap their fingers as they rap around the room.

HOPE RAP

Some people hope the rains will fall;
Others hope their friends might call—
Some people put their hope in money,
But that kinda hope will fail you, honey!

(chorus) *So I put my hopes far up above me,*
In my God who knows and loves me!
For what God has promised will come true,
And heavenly hope won't disappoint you!

Some people hope they'll pass the test,
Others hope they'll find some rest—
Some people put their hope in "rabbit-foots,"
But that kinda hope will fail you, toots!
(Repeat chorus)

Lesson 13

Then say: **Wow! What a great way to get revved up about the hope we have in the Lord! And the words to our rap are so true—our futures are so bright with hope from God. We've spent several weeks exploring hope and where it comes from. We've learned that hope from God is hope that never disappoints us. And we've discovered that even through suffering and tough times, God helps us grow strong hope to last a lifetime.**

Today we'll end our study of hope by making cool Cookie Calendars to remind us of the hope we have every day of our lives. Later we'll decorate real cookies to give others as reminders of placing their hope in the Lord. Right now, let's review some important things we've learned about hope. These cookie sheets will help! Distribute the cookie sheets.

THE MIGHTY MESSAGE

Have colored vinyl tape, permanent markers, magnetic strip, and scissors handy for kids to use during this review activity. You'll also need to cut 2-by-6-inch posterboard strips. Cut six strips for each child.

Have kids form small groups and hand each group scissors and several rolls of colored tape. Say: **I'll read a verse, then ask a question or two. When you know the answers, gently tap on your cookie sheets. Then we'll add colorful touches to the sheets as we discuss the answers.**

Read aloud Job 11:18; Psalm 25:5; and Hebrews 10:23. Ask:

★ **Who gives us hope we can trust?**

★ **How does knowing God keeps his promises help us have hope?**

After kids have answered, have them place one or two tape strips up the left sides of the cookie sheets and use permanent markers to write, "Be a smart cookie..." on the tape. Say: **Smart cookies do place their hope in God because they know hope comes from God and his Word! Now let's see how Jesus gives us living hope and an eternal future with God.** Read aloud 1 Peter 1:3, 4 and Titus 1:2. Ask:

★ **In what ways did Jesus' birth bring us hope?**

POWER POINTERS

Photocopy all the Mighty Memory Verses from page 127 on bright neon paper for kids to practice at home. Remember: reinforcement means memory!

Lesson 13

★ **What hope does Jesus give us through his death and resurrection?**

After kids respond by tapping on their cookie sheets and discussing the answers, add one or two tape strips up the right sides of the cookie sheets and write, "Hope in the Lord!' up the strips using permanent markers.

Say: **Jesus' birth, death, and resurrection give us the hope of forgiveness and eternal life with God. We have a living hope in Jesus because when we accept him and hope in his love, we can be forgiven and have eternal life in heaven. Next, let's review what we've learned about having hope for tomorrow.** Read aloud Proverbs 23:18; Isaiah 40:31; and Jeremiah 29:11; 31:17a. Ask:

★ **What did God promise us?**

★ **Why does God keep his promises to us?**

When both questions have been answered, add a colored-tape X to each cookie sheet, running diagonally from corner to corner. Then say: **Isn't it wonderful to know that God has promised us a hope and a future and that God will keep his promise? We never have to be without hope when we love and trust God! Now we'll review how we can find hope in this often hopeless world.** Read aloud Ephesians 2:10 and Hebrews 10:24, then ask:

★ **How can serving God and others help us have stronger hope? help others have hope?**

Have kids add tape lines down and across the centers of their cookie sheets. Say: **We find hope in many ways: through serving God, by helping others, through prayer and reading the Bible, and through trusting God even in hard times. When we love and obey God, we're never without hope, and his hope will never disappoint us. Why, there's enough hope to carry us through every day and every month of the year! Let's make strips with the names of the months on them to remind us how the hope God gives us lasts all year through, year after year.**

Hand each child six poster-board strips. Write the abbreviations for each month on the strips in pairs. For example, write "Jan." on one side of a strip and "Feb."

119

Lesson 13

on the flip side. Stick a small half-inch square of self-adhesive magnetic strip to each side of the strips so they will stick at the tops of the metal cookie sheets. Let kids place the correct monthly label at the tops of their Cookie Calendars.

Say: **Your Cookie Calendars are looking awesome! Isn't it great having hope that lasts every day, month after month? Let's see if we can spread some of this wonderful hope to others and remind them to be smart cookies who place their hope in the Lord!**

THE MESSAGE IN MOTION

Before class, collect packaged cookies (two for each child), canned or tube icing, candy sprinkles, plastic sandwich bags, twist-tie wires, adhesive picture hangers, and copies of the Smart Cookie strip below. You'll also need glue and copies of the Smart Cookie Calendar page. (For larger copies, photocopy and enlarge the Smart Cookie Calendar page on 11-by-17 paper.)

Invite kids to work in pairs or trios and each decorate two cookies: one to eat later and one to share. Have each child place one of his decorated cookies in a plastic sandwich bag and seal it with a twist-tie wire. Tape a Smart Cookie strip to each bag. Have kids take their sweet reminders of hope in the Lord to another class. Invite a volunteer from your class to tell why putting hope in the Lord is the smart thing to do, then read aloud 2 Thessalonians 2:16, 17 to the class.

When you return to your room, let kids enjoy their sweet treats as you discuss what life would be like if we were hopeless and didn't have the Lord to love and help us. Point out that when we love and obey the Lord, we always have hope that never disappoints us—today and every day. Then have kids glue copies of the calendar page to the centers of their Cookie Calendars and glue the picture hangers to the backs of the cookie sheets.

Read aloud Lamentations 3:21-23, then say: **God gives us fresh hope every day, and that's important to remember. We can awaken each day with new hope in God and in his power to help and love us. Now let's finish our Cookie Calendars as we review the Mighty Memory Verses we've learned over the last several weeks.**

BE A SMART COOKIE...
PLACE YOUR HOPE IN THE LORD!
(Hebrews 10:23)

Lesson 13

SUPER SCRIPTURE

Before class, cut out several heart patterns from poster board or old file folders. Kids will each make one large heart and three smaller hearts to use on their calendars. You'll also need poster board, markers, and self-adhesive magnetic strip for this activity.

Have kids trace and cut out poster-board hearts and color them red. Have each child prepare one large paper heart and three smaller hearts. Cut small squares of self-adhesive magnetic strip to fit on the backs of the hearts. As kids work, remind them that it's important to learn, remember, and use God's Word because it brings us hope.

When the hearts are complete, let kids stick them to the bottom portion of their Cookie Calendars. Say: **We can use your Cookie Calendars to play a game that will help us review the four Mighty Memory Verses we've learned in the last few weeks. Let's form four teams.** Have kids get into four teams, then say: **I'll repeat one of the Mighty Memory Verses. When you find that verse on your Cookie Calendar, stick a paper heart to the square and raise your hand. The first team with a hand in the air can read the verse aloud and will score a "smart cookie" point.**

One by one, repeat the following four Mighty Memory Verses from the previous weeks.

★ *"Be strong and take heart, all you who hope in the* Lord.*" Psalm 31:24*
★ *"There is surely a future hope for you, and your hope will not be cut off." Proverbs 23:18*
★ *"We have this hope as an anchor for the soul, firm and secure." Hebrews 6:19*
★ *"Let us hold unswervingly to the hope we profess, for he who promised is faithful." Hebrews 10:23*

When kids have marked all four Mighty Memory Verses with the paper hearts, challenge the teams to repeat each verse without looking. Score one extra bonus point for each verse correctly repeated. Have the winning team give high fives to the other teams.

Lesson 13

Say: **You remembered these verses well, and they will help you hold on to the hope God freely gives us. You can use the small hearts to mark your favorite verses on the calendars. Use your big paper hearts to mark the days of each month. You can change the names of the months using the poster-board strips with the names of the month on them. Each day of every month there's something to read, do, or repeat that will remind you of the hope we have in the Lord and how his hope never leaves us or disappoints us. Now let's end our together time with a prayer thanking God for such perfect, heavenly hope!**

A POWERFUL PROMISE

Have kids set their Cookie Calendars aside and sit in a circle. Say: **For several weeks we've learned how God, Jesus, and the Holy Spirit all work to give us hope and help us hold on to hope. We've discovered that heavenly hope is different from everyday hopes, such as when we say, "I hope it doesn't rain." Heavenly hope is hope from God and is based on the loving promises he gives us to be near us, love us, help and guide us, and offer us forgiveness and eternal life in heaven. Heavenly hope will never disappoint us or fade away. It's hope we can count on day after day and is fresh each morning!**

Hold up the Bible and say: **God's Word contains his loving, powerful promises, and God has promised us a hope and a future we can count on. We can make our own promises to God to seek his help and hold on to the hope he gives us. We'll pass the Bible around the circle. When you receive the Bible, you can say, "Lord, please help me always hold on to your hope and help."** After everyone has held the Bible, end with a prayer thanking God for the hope we can count on day after day our whole lives through. Close with a corporate "amen."

Lead kids in the Hope Rap from page 117 once more as you clap and snap your way around the room. Then read aloud Lamentations 3:21-23. End with this responsive good-bye:

Leader: **May God's hope live in your hearts forever!**

Children: **And also in you!**

Remind kids to take home their Cookie Calendars and mark the days as they remember the power there is in God's heavenly hope. Thank children for coming and encourage them to keep their promises to God this week.

CHRISTMAS STAR PATTERNS

© 2001 by Susan L. Lingo.
Permission is granted to reproduce this page for ministry purposes only—not for resale.

FUTURE CARDS

There is surely a future hope for you, and your hope will not be cut off. Proverbs 23:18	For we are God's workmanship, created in Christ Jesus to do good works, which God prepared in advance for us to do. Ephesians 2:10
"For I know the plans I have for you," declares the LORD, "plans to prosper you and not to harm you, plans to give you hope and a future." Jeremiah 29:11	A faith and knowledge resting on the hope of eternal life, which God, who does not lie, promised before the beginning of time. Titus 1:2
"So there is hope for your future," declares the LORD. Jeremiah 31:17	In my Father's house are many rooms; if it were not so, I would have told you. I am going there to prepare a place for you. John 14:2

COOL SHADES PATTERNS

© 2001 by Susan L. Lingo.
Permission is granted to reproduce this page for ministry purposes only—not for resale.

RIGHT ON TARGET VERSES

#1: SUFFERING. We also rejoice in our sufferings. (Romans 5:3)

#1: SUFFERING. We also rejoice in our sufferings. (Romans 5:3)

#2: PERSEVERANCE. Wait for the LORD; be strong and take heart and wait for the LORD. (Psalm 27:14)

#2: PERSEVERANCE. Wait for the LORD; be strong and take heart and wait for the LORD. (Psalm 27:14)

#3: CHARACTER. I wait for the LORD, my soul waits, and in his word I put my hope. (Psalm 130:5)

#3: CHARACTER. I wait for the LORD, my soul waits, and in his word I put my hope. (Psalm 130:5)

#4: HOPE. We wait in hope for the LORD; he is our help and our shield. In him our hearts rejoice, for we trust in his holy name. (Psalm 33:20, 21)

#4: HOPE. We wait in hope for the LORD; he is our help and our shield. In him our hearts rejoice, for we trust in his holy name. (Psalm 33:20, 21)

© 2001 by Susan L. Lingo.
Permission is granted to reproduce this page for ministry purposes only—not for resale.

SMART COOKIE CALENDAR

1. "Be strong and take heart, all you who hope in the Lord" (Psalm 31:24).

2. Say something encouraging to a friend today.

3. Hope never disappoints us.

4. When we love and obey God, we find hope.

5. Read Hebrews 10:23 today.

6. Each time you see a bird today, silently say: "I have God's hope!"

7. Thank God for helping you hold on to hope today.

8. Serve someone in a secret way today.

9. Read Psalm 23 before bed.

10. "There is surely a future hope for you, and your hope will not be cut off" (Proverbs 23:18).

11. Use the word *hope* in a sentence today.

12. Write a note telling God what you need hope for.

13. Take a walk and thank God for your bright day!

14. Give a family member a note about our hope in God.

15. "We have this hope as an anchor for the soul, firm and secure" (Hebrews 6:19).

16. Read Lamentations 3:21-23.

17. Draw the way hope feels in your heart.

18. Each time you smile today, remember the hope in your heart.

19. List all that you have to be hopeful for.

20. Read John 14:1-3. Draw a picture of your home of hope Jesus is preparing.

21. Invite a friend to sit with you at lunch. Share all you're glad for.

22. Thank God for the little things in your life.

23. Slip a happy note under a family member's pillow.

24. Thank the Holy Spirit for being with you.

25. Make a family list of all you have to be hopeful for this week.

26. Write Proverbs 23:18 on a slip of paper. Secretly hand it to a friend.

27. Each time you see the color blue, think: *My hope is in the Lord!*

28. "Wait for the Lord; be strong and take heart and wait for the Lord" (Psalm 27:14).

29. "Let us hold unswervingly to the hope we profess, for he who promised is faithful" Hebrews 10:23.

30. Call someone on the phone and tell them you're thankful for them.

31. "Then you will know that I am the Lord; those who hope in me will not be disappointed" (Isaiah 49:23).

© 2001 by Susan L. Lingo.
Permission is granted to reproduce this page for ministry purposes only—not for resale.

SCRIPTURE STRIPS

Be strong and take heart, all you who hope in the LORD. *Psalm 31:24*

But as for me, I watch in hope for the LORD, I wait for God my Savior; my God will hear me. *Micah 7:7*

There is surely a future hope for you, and your hope will not be cut off. *Proverbs 23:18*

"For I know the plans I have for you," declares the LORD, "plans to prosper you and not to harm you, plans to give you hope and a future." *Jeremiah 29:11*

We have this hope as an anchor for the soul, firm and secure. *Hebrews 6:19*

Because of the LORD's great love we are not consumed, for his compassions never fail. They are new every morning. *Lamentations 3:22, 23a*

Let us hold unswervingly to the hope we profess, for he who promised is faithful. *Hebrews 10:23*

Now faith is being sure of what we hope for and certain of what we do not see. *Hebrews 11:1*

POWER UP YOUR KIDS!

Now there are eight Power Builders books to empower your kids for a lifetime of faith! Susan Lingo's Power Builders curriculum engages kids in learning as much as in fun! Each topical 13-lesson book includes Bible-bound, Scripture-sound, kid-pleasing, life-changing lessons—PLUS teacher training and ways to tell if your kids are really learning. What a powerful combination!

Value Seekers
(42111)
Help kids transform their lives by seeking, recognizing, and living by the values Jesus taught.

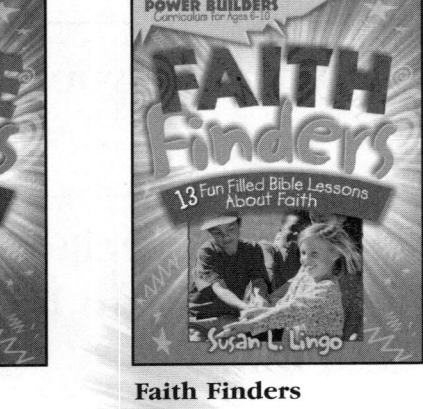

Faith Finders
(42112)
Direct kids to discover their own faith in God through Jesus and the Holy Spirit.

Servant Leaders
(42113)
Motivate kids to develop a life-long attitude of serving God and others by examining the lives of Bible times servants.

Disciple Makers
(42114)
Lead kids to know more about Jesus and equip them to follow Jesus and to disciple others.

Power Boosters
(42115)
Empower your kids by helping them discover God's power to change their lives.

Peace Makers
(42116)
Build your kids' abilities to be at peace with God, others, and themselves.

Joy Builders
(42117)
Encourage kids to discover the joy of the Lord and to build on that joy by getting to know Jesus more and more.

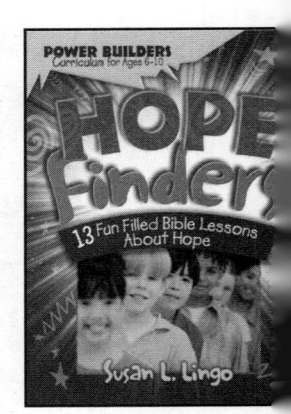

Hope Finders
(42118)
Share the hope kids find in knowing and obeying God and help them live with an eternal hope.

Look for these and other excellent Christian education products by Standard Publishing at your local Christian bookstore or order directly from Standard Publishing by calling 1-800-482-2060.